BE CYBER SMART

Satyendra 'Satyen' K. Dwivedi is a technology expert with three decades of extensive experience, having consistently spearheaded innovative, secure and scalable digital systems. His impactful career spans leadership roles at industry giants such as Mahindra Group, Oracle and Infosys, alongside numerous dynamic start-ups. An alumnus of IIT-Kanpur and IIM-Bangalore, Satyen has served as CTO for prominent organisations, including Mahindra Holidays, Mahindra Retail, Babyoye and HolidayIQ.com. *Be Cyber Smart* is his first book.

SATYENDRA K. DWIVEDI

BE CYBER SMART

AN ESSENTIAL GUIDE FOR EVERY INDIAN

Published by Westland Books, a division of Nasadiya Technologies Private Limited, in 2025

No. 269/2B, First Floor, 'Irai Arul', Vimalraj Street, Nethaji Nagar, Alapakkam Main Road, Maduravoyal, Chennai 600095

Westland and the Westland logo are the trademarks of Nasadiya Technologies Private Limited, or its affiliates.

ISBN: 9789371977449

10 9 8 7 6 5 4 3 2 1

Typeset by Jojy Philip

Printed at Parksons Graphics Pvt. Ltd

This book is dedicated to the courageous individuals who shared their cyber scam experiences; their powerful stories were the inspiration for this work.

To every Indian family striving for digital safety, may this guide empower you to be truly cyber smart.

Contents

Introduction

TWO SIDES OF THE DIGITAL COIN

I am very glad that you have picked up this book. I know your time is valuable. But trust me, this knowledge is very important for the current digital environment. It is an investment of your time that you won't regret.

You see, India is changing very fast. Just think back a few years. Remember when we only had landlines, and calling someone far away was a big deal, a special occasion? Now, everyone has a smartphone. From young kids making those catchy 'reels' that go viral to parents confidently using UPI for everything—paying for groceries, sending money to relatives in another city, even donating to a temple—the internet is everywhere! It's not just a tool anymore; it's woven into the very fabric of our daily lives. It's like a big, bustling market full of wonderful things and new possibilities. You can learn new recipes from all over the world, connect with old school friends you haven't seen in ages, watch your favourite cricket teams play live and even pay your electricity bill instantly, all from the comfort of your home.

This digital revolution, while bringing immense opportunities, also brings challenges. Just like any crowded place or busy market, there are some not-so-good people here too. They are like clever pickpockets, but their target is your information, your hard-earned money as well as your peace of mind. We call this dark side 'cybercrime'. And sadly, it's growing very fast in India. It's a new kind of thief that operates not in person but from behind a screen, often from far away, using clever tricks to trap unsuspecting people.

I understand that sometimes we Indians are a bit trusting or naive. We think everyone is good-hearted, that people generally mean well. And honestly, it's a beautiful quality, a core part of our culture. But on the internet, this very quality can make us vulnerable. These cyber criminals prey on our trust and helpful nature. And, let's be honest, not everyone in the family knows how to use mobile applications and online services wisely. Young ones, the Gen Z and Gen Alpha, might be born with a smartphone in their hands, effortlessly swiping and typing. But elders, parents or grandparents, often find it all a bit confusing, a bit overwhelming. They might struggle with remembering complex passwords or identifying a malicious message. And that's entirely understandable.

The digital world is new to many of us, and learning takes time. Sometimes, that learning comes at a very high cost—like losing our hard-earned savings.

WHY THIS BOOK, WHY NOW?

Let me tell you a true and chilling story from March 2025. An eighty-six-year-old woman in Mumbai was enjoying her peaceful golden years when she received a phone call that changed everything. The caller claimed to be a high-ranking officer from the Central Bureau of Investigation (CBI). He told her that her Aadhaar card had been linked to a major money laundering case and she was now under 'digital arrest'. He instructed her not to hang up or tell anyone, warning that her children would be arrested if she did.

The scammer then forced her into a video call. On her screen, she saw a man dressed in a police uniform, seated in what looked like a police station, complete with police radio transmission sounds. He showed her fake documents, even a fake arrest warrant with her name on it, and threatened to freeze her bank accounts and ruin her family's reputation. He made her believe that if she left her house or spoke to anyone, real police would immediately arrest her.

For two terrifying months, this elderly woman was held prisoner in her own home, constantly on calls with these criminals. They made her believe that she was undergoing an 'e-investigation' as part of the 'Digital India Movement'.

Through a mix of sweet talk and threats, they tricked her into giving them access to all her bank details, her fixed deposits and even information about her property. Under immense stress and desperate to protect her family, she kept transferring money. First, smaller amounts, then larger ones, for made-up 'court fees', 'investigation charges' and to 'clear her name'.

Bit by bit, her entire life's savings, built up over decades, disappeared. Her children's inheritance, her peace of mind—all gone. In those two months, she lost a shocking ₹20.25 crore.

Eventually, her domestic help noticed her strange behaviour—staying locked in her room, yelling into the phone. Finally, her daughter intervened, and they went to the real police. The truth was heartbreaking: the money was gone, transferred to countless accounts and likely converted into cryptocurrency, making it almost impossible to recover.

This is the harsh reality of these scams. They are carefully planned attacks that use fear and isolation to steal everything from innocent people. These criminals are ruthless and don't care about their victims' age or weaknesses. In these circumstances, we all need to be extremely careful and aware of these terrible tactics. Let's learn about these scams and protect ourselves and our loved ones from such shocking frauds.

The purpose of this book is simple yet critical: to help Indian families stay safe online. I want to share with you the practical knowledge and the simple, actionable tips you need to navigate this digital landscape with confidence. Think of me as your friendly neighbourhood adviser, here to guide you, not with complicated technical terms, but with relatable examples and easy-to-understand explanations. We'll break down complex topics into small pieces, just like a grandmother explaining a complicated recipe step-by-step.

The book will talk about all sorts of things that directly affect us here in India. To start, we'll discuss how to keep your UPI payments safe from fraudsters who might send you fake requests, and explore what to look out for on social media platforms like WhatsApp, Facebook and Instagram, where fake news and phishing links often spread like wildfire. We will also talk about catchy messages, and the potential dangers behind them, and cover how to explain these digital dangers to children, who are glued to their screens for entertainment and education, and how to set healthy boundaries for them.

This book isn't just a generic guide. It's specifically tailored for us Indians, and considers our unique tech context. The incredible prevalence of UPI that makes digital payments accessible to crores, also makes it a prime target for scams. The boom of social media and short videos like reels has transformed how we communicate and consume media, but it has also brought challenges like cybercrime and the spread of misinformation.

The book also recognises the varying levels of digital literacy across our diverse populations. What might be obvious to a tech-savvy youngster might be completely new territory for someone who's only recently started using a smartphone. And yes, we'll address that inherent cultural element of trust and naivety that, while beautiful, can be exploited by criminals. The goal is to empower you to recognise, to question and to protect yourself without losing your core values.

In the following pages, we'll learn about our digital identity and untangle the thought process of cyber criminals. I will also share many stories of scams from the news, or those inspired by current events. The purpose of these isn't to scare you, but to help you understand the various technologies and methods scammers use. The more aware you are, the safer you'll be! In the last chapters, we'll talk about how to protect ourselves, and if anything goes wrong, what should be done to minimise the loss.

This book is for every Indian family. Whether you live in a city with high-speed internet or in a village with occasional connectivity. Whether you're a tech guru who understands every application or someone who's just starting their online journey, this is for you. For students, homemakers, professionals, or retired seniors, the information here is relevant and important.

My hope is that by the end of this book, you will feel more confident, aware and better equipped to protect yourself from online threats. By learning together, sharing experiences and building a stronger, safer digital community, we'll make our online lives as secure, joyful and prosperous as our offline ones.

So, are you ready? Let's begin this essential journey to a safer digital India together.

Part One

THE DIGITAL WORLD AND ITS RISKS

CHAPTER ONE

Your Digital Identity

In this chapter, we're going to talk about something very important, your digital information and how you live your life online.

Do you know what 'personal information' means in today's world? It's not just your name or address anymore; it's much more. Think about it: when you go online, you share a lot. That includes your phone number, email ID, date of birth, Aadhaar number, PAN card details, bank account number, debit or credit card details and even your UPI ID. All of this is personal information.

And what about your photos? The ones you share on WhatsApp or Instagram? Those are considered personal information too. Even videos, voice recordings, status and your location data. If your phone knows where you are, that's personal information.

Think about your health details. If you use a fitness app or a smartwatch, it collects data. Many phones use your fingerprints and your facial recognition data. This is all your personal information.

In India, more and more of our lives have become digital. We pay bills online, shop online, talk to friends and family online and even get government services online. This means that a significant amount of our personal information is online, across many different websites and apps.

YOUR DIGITAL FOOTPRINT

Have you heard of a 'digital footprint'? It may sound a bit technical, but it's actually very simple. Imagine you're walking on sand, you're bound to leave footprints, right? A digital footprint is similar. It's the trail you leave behind whenever you use the internet.

Every time you go online, you leave a mark. When you visit a website, post a comment, like a photo, buy something online or send an email—all these actions create a digital footprint.

This footprint grows bigger every day. It includes everything about your online presence: your searches, browsing or shopping history, your social media posts, the apps you download and even the jokes you share!

Why is this important? Because this footprint tells a story about you. It shows what you like, what you do, where you go and who your friends are. It can even show what you believe in.

Think about it, if someone looks at your footprint, they can learn a lot about you—sometimes, more than you realise. It's like leaving clues about yourself everywhere you go. And once something is online, it's very difficult to remove. It stays there, sometimes forever. So, think before you post;

think before you share. Because your digital footprint is permanent. It has implications—it can affect your future, your job and your relationships.

—~—

YOUR DATA IS GOLD

You might think, 'Why would anyone want my data? I'm not important.' But believe me, your data is very, very valuable. To cyber criminals, it's like gold (even marketers are after this gold).

Why? Because they can use it to harm you, and to make money. Here are some ways your data can be used to land you in trouble:

- Identity Theft: This is quite common. They steal your personal details, like your Aadhaar, PAN or bank details. Then they pretend to be you. They can open bank accounts in your name. They can take loans. They can even commit crimes. And you might be the one held responsible.
- Financial Fraud: With your bank details or card numbers, they can empty your bank account, make purchases online or transfer your money elsewhere. This happens very quickly. You might get an SMS about a transaction you didn't make and by then, it might be too late.
- Phishing and Scams: They use your email ID or phone number to call or send you fake messages. Pretending to be your bank, or a government official or a trusted company, they try to trick you into sharing information,

or paying money or clicking on a malicious link. Once you click on it, your phone or computer can get infected and they can steal even more of your data.

- Blackmail and Extortion: They might get a hold of your private photos or videos, sensitive conversations or browsing history. They might even make a new photo or video using different technology. Then they threaten to make this media public, unless you pay them money.
- Targeting Your Loved Ones: If they know about your family, they can target them too. They might send fake messages to your parents, or to your children pretending to be you in trouble, asking for money, or asking for information.
- Misinformation and Defamation: They can use your accounts to spread false information, or post things that damage your reputation. They can make you look bad, harming your job, your social life and your good name.

So, you see, your data is not just numbers and words. It's a key, that in the hands if the wrong person, can unlock many problems for you. Which is why protecting it is crucial.

PROTECTING PRIVACY

We all use social media: Facebook, Instagram, WhatsApp and many other apps. These platforms have 'privacy settings', but how do you use them? These settings are very important. They let you control who sees your information, including your photos, who can send you messages and who can see your location.

Think about it: if your profile is 'public', anyone can see your posts, download your photos and know exactly where you are, which is very risky. Here are some reasons why protecting your privacy is important:

- Personal Safety: If strangers know too much about you, it can be dangerous. They might know when you're not home or where your children go to school, which can lead to real-world threats.
- Financial Security: Cyber criminals are always looking for data to scam people. Strong privacy settings make it harder for them to find your details and gather information that can lead to fraud.
- Reputation Management: What you share online stays online. Even if you delete it, it might still be out there. Strong privacy settings help you control your image and prevent unwanted people from seeing your private life.

Protecting Children

This is perhaps the most important point. Our children are growing up in a highly digital world. They might not understand its dangers and could end up sharing information without thinking. It's our responsibility to protect them.

- Teach Them about Privacy: Explain to them what personal information is. Tell them not to share their full name, address, school name or phone number online.
- Monitor Their Online Activity: It's not about spying; it's about guiding them. Understand what apps they use and who they talk to.

- Set Strong Privacy Settings on Their Accounts: If they have social media, make sure their profiles are private. Only trusted friends should be able to see their posts.
- Educate Them about Online Strangers: Tell them not to talk to strangers online or meet anyone they met online in person.
- Beware of Cyberbullying: Children can be cruel, and online platforms can make it worse. Teach your children to be kind, and if they face bullying, to inform you immediately.
- Think Before They Share: Tell your children to take a moment to evaluate their post. Would it make them uncomfortable if their grandparents or a favourite teacher looked at it? If it does, that's a good sign it shouldn't go online. The safety of our children, both online and offline, is our priority.

The digital world is a powerful tool. It connects us, entertains us, but it also has its dark side. By understanding these risks and taking small steps, we can protect ourselves and our families. We can enjoy the benefits of the digital world without falling prey to its dangers. Always remember, a little caution goes a long way. Stay safe, stay smart!

CHAPTER TWO

Cyber Attacks on Our Families

Sometimes, just hearing the word 'cybercrime' can make us feel quite worried. It isn't just a crime about big companies or government secrets; it can be very personal too. It reaches right into our homes, and our families can often be the targets. But don't let that fear take over. Here, we're going to discuss how cyber thieves actually work, what their tricks are, why our families are easy targets, and most importantly, how we can protect ourselves from them. It's not complicated; it's all about being switched on, being aware.

WHAT DO THESE CRIMINALS WANT?

Now, let's try to understand why scammers do such things. Understanding their motives helps us be more aware of their strategies.

To Earn Money: This is the biggest driver. Most cybercrimes happen for money.

- Easy Targets: They look for people who are less familiar with the internet, or those who might not be very tech-savvy.
- Luring with Greed: They play on our desires. They tempt you with promises of lottery wins, big prizes, expensive gifts, investments, easy money or incredibly cheap deals—all to lure you into their trap.

To Take Revenge: Sometimes, people commit cybercrime out of a desire for revenge.

- Personal Enmity: If there's a personal fight or an old grievance, people sometimes try to take revenge online.
- Venting Anger: Some people use the internet to vent their anger. Without much thought, they target anyone they feel like bothering.

For Fun/Mischief: Some individuals do these things just for the kicks, or to show off their so-called 'power'.

- Show-Off: They want to impress their friends, to show how 'smart' and 'big' a hacker they are.
- Passing Time: Believe it or not, some people just do it to pass the time, or because they are bored.

And yes, there are also organised crime gangs. They have entire networks. Certain regions in India have become notorious as cybercrime hubs for these groups. They work together to commit these crimes on a large scale. Being aware of their different motives can help you anticipate their moves.

One more crucial point to understand: the internet has no boundaries. These cyber thieves can be anywhere in the world. Cyber thieves from many countries, i.e., South Asia, Southeast Asia and Africa, do target Indians. When they are in another country, it becomes very difficult for our police to catch them. Law enforcement agencies need to coordinate internationally. This takes extensive time and effort.

But regardless of where they are, the impact is directly on us. Our money is lost, our reputation is harmed and our peace of mind is disturbed. This is precisely why our personal awareness becomes so important. Since it's hard for the authorities to catch them quickly, we must be our first line of defence.

WHY INDIAN FAMILIES ARE TARGETED

We understood what cybercrime is and how it's growing. Now, let's get into something important. Why are we, our very own Indian families, easy targets? It's not our fault. It's not because we are not sharp. There are other factors and we need to understand them.

Our Trusting Nature

Think about our culture. We are generally taught to trust. We respect elders. We believe what people tell us, especially if they seem to be from a good background, or from a government office or a big company. This is a central part of being Indian. It makes our society strong as we help each other and rely on each other.

But sadly, cyber criminals take advantage of this. They know we can be trusting. They know we respect authority. So, they pretend to be from banks, or from the police or from the income tax department. They sound official, use big words, and because we tend to respect such people, we listen. We follow instructions even if those instructions sound a little off. We think, 'Oh, they must know best.' This is called 'social engineering'. It's when someone tricks you into doing something by playing with your feelings and trust. It's like someone wearing a uniform and asking for your house keys. You might just give it because they look official. It's a sad reality, but our trusting nature can sometimes be used against us.

Different Ages, Different Understandings

In our homes, we have seniors, we have adults and then we have the youngsters. Everyone uses smartphones and the internet. But do we all use it in the same way? Do we all understand it in the same way? Not really.

Our seniors might be new to this digital world. They might not know what an one-time password (OTP) is, or why they should never share it. They might click on any link that comes, or believe any message that promises a lot of money, or a message which says that your account will be closed. They are only trying to keep up. They want to connect with their grandchildren. They want to watch videos. But they don't have the same 'digital sense' as someone who grew up with computers.

Then there are adults. They use UPI and do online banking. They are comfortable. But even they could miss a trick, by forgetting to check a website address properly, or because they don't know how to spot a fake call. They are very busy. They are just trying to earn a living and don't have time to learn about new online risks.

And the youngsters? They are online all the time. They know social media. They know games. But even they can fall for traps. Like fake job offers. Or online gaming scams. Or blackmail. They might share too much personal information. They might be too eager to trust someone they meet online. While they may be digitally literate, they don't have enough life experience to deal with professional scammers. So, you see, digital literacy is not the same for everyone in our families. This difference creates gaps and criminals exploit these gaps.

New Tech, No Awareness

We are all getting smartphones. We are all on WhatsApp. And we all use payment apps. India is booming digitally. Which is good for us as it can make life easier. But with this speed, comes a problem.

We adopt new technologies very fast. But we don't always get enough information about the risks. It's like buying a new, powerful car but no one teaches us how to drive it safely. We are just given the keys, we start driving. And then accidents happen.

Think about QR code scams. Many of us use QR codes to pay. It's so simple: just scan and pay. But criminals put up misleading QR codes which take you to malicious websites, or send you a QR code through which they can steal money. We don't think twice before we scan because we trust the technology. We don't realise that bad people can also manipulate this technology. Often, we don't even read the terms and conditions or check for security updates. The criminals love this. They wait for us to make mistakes.

Online Payments: So Convenient, So Risky

UPI, net banking, mobile wallets—we use them for everything. From buying vegetables to paying school fees. It's convenient. There's no need for cash. No need to stand in queues. This is a revolution for India.

But with this convenience comes risk. Every online transaction is a door and if that door is not locked properly, someone can get in. Criminals target these transactions by sending fake payment requests or pretending to be customer care. They say your UPI is blocked, or your bank account is frozen. By creating a sense of urgency, they make you panic.

And because we do so many online payments, we become complacent about them. We don't always check every detail. Is the merchant's name correct? Is the amount I'm paying right? Is the transaction message from my actual bank? We just click. We just type. And then, poof, the money is gone.

Old Scams, New Clothes

Remember the old days? Someone would call you and say that you won a lottery, or a big prize, and you just had to pay a small 'processing fee' to get it. Or someone would come to your door and try to sell you something fake.

Those old scams have just moved online. They are wearing new clothes now. That lottery call? It's now an SMS, or a WhatsApp message, saying you won lakhs of rupees. And you just need to click a link, or share your bank details. That fake job offer? It's now on LinkedIn, or a social media ad, asking for a 'registration fee', or your Aadhaar card details.

Even the 'relative in trouble' scam, where someone calls saying your family member is in an accident and needs money urgently, used to be a phone call. Now it's a desperate message from a fake WhatsApp number with a reliable-looking profile picture, or a hacked social media account. They use the same old tricks, but with more data to make us trust them.

This is why we are targeted. It's a mix of our cultural values, our different comfort levels with technology, our eagerness to adopt new things and the shift of old tricks to new platforms. It's a lot to take in. But understanding the fundamentals of cybercrimes is the first step to how we can protect ourselves. Scammers will keep innovating, but as long as we understand their motives and the style of their operations, we can protect ourselves. Knowing what's out there is half the battle won.

In the next few chapters, we are going to discuss different types of scams that are happening in India. These chapters will have stories which are real or inspired by real stories. They tell of people who lost their hard-earned money, which is not meant to scare you, but to make you aware, and to make you understand these or similar scams so that you don't fall into the same trap. You will be surprised to know there are so many types of scams. Remember, awareness is our strongest shield.

Part Two

SCAM STORIES

CHAPTER THREE

The Danger of Nasty Links

Our money, our hard-earned money, and how some clever, bad people try to snatch it away. With just a click on a malicious link! Let's try to understand their tricks to stay safe.

Our phones and computers afford us a lot of convenience, but this ease also brings risks. Many scams start with a simple link. This link can come in an email, WhatsApp message, SMS or in social media apps. Just one click, and poof! Your money is gone.

I understand how scary this can feel. But once you know their ways, you can fight back. So, let's dive into some stories. Stories that happened to people just like us. And then, we'll see how we can avoid such troubles.

PHISHING: THE AUTO-DEBIT TRAP

You're waiting for your electricity bill, or maybe a refund from an online purchase and suddenly, you get an SMS or an email. It looks very official. It says, 'Your bill payment is due. Click here to avoid disconnection.' Or, 'Your refund is pending. Click here to get it.' You get short, simple messages. 'You've won a lottery! Click here to claim.' The link takes you to a fake website that looks very real. You click on the page, and sometimes without even entering an OTP, your money is gone.

Many people in Delhi got SMS messages about pending electricity bills. They appeared so real. One lady, Priya, clicked the link. The page that opened looked exactly like the electricity board's website. She just wanted to pay her bill and within minutes, ₹25,000 was debited from her bank account. She was shocked! She had no idea how it had happened. It was an unauthorised payment link and the money went to the fraudsters.

Back in February 2024, many people in an Indian city received SMS messages about winning a huge lottery. One young student, Rahul, got excited by this. The message said he had won ₹50 lakh! He clicked the link, which led to a page asking for his bank account number and an 'advance processing fee' of ₹5,000. He paid it, hoping for the big win. But, of course, the lottery was fake, and his ₹5,000 was gone. He felt completely foolish.

What Could Have Helped

- Always Check the Sender's Information: Was the SMS from an official number? Usually, companies send messages from a sender ID like 'EB-BSES' or 'HP-GAS'. NOT a random mobile number.
- Don't Click Links in Suspicious Messages: If you need to pay a bill, go directly to the official website of the company. Type the website address yourself. Don't use a link from an SMS or email.

- Verify, Verify, Verify: If you're unsure, contact the company's customer care service. Their official number is usually available on their website or your old bills.
- Too Good to Be True: If it sounds too good to be true, it probably is! Lotteries you didn't enter, huge discounts on things you didn't buy ... these are usually scams.
- Never Pay to Receive a Prize: No legitimate lottery or company will ask you to pay a fee to claim a prize.

YOUR KYC SECRETS

These scams often involve a message, an email or even a call telling you that your bank account or SIM card will be blocked if you don't update your 'Know Your Customer' (KYC) details. Similar to the auto-debit trap, they send you a website like which leads to a fake page designed to steal your details. They want your bank account details, your Aadhaar number, your PAN card number; all your sensitive information! They create a sense of urgency and fear to make you act without thinking. It's a classic trick, but still so effective.

In July 2024, a businessman, Mr Sharma, got an email from what appeared to be his bank. 'Your KYC is pending. Update it to continue banking services.' The email had a link and Mr Sharma clicked it. The website looked identical to his bank's login page, so he entered his username, password and even his debit card details. He thought he was doing the right thing. Within an hour, ₹1.5 lakh were siphoned off from his bank account. He was heartbroken. All his personal details were now with the fraudsters.

In March 2025, a thirty-eight-year-old chartered accountant from Pune received a WhatsApp message, seemingly from the 'ICICI Bank KYC team'. The message said his account would be disabled if he didn't update his KYC details by the end of the day. It even had a PDF attachment. When he opened the file, he was taken to a web page that looked exactly like his bank's official website. He put in his customer ID and phone number, thinking he needed an OTP to proceed. A few minutes later, he was kicked out of his own WhatsApp account. Immediately, his friends and clients started getting messages from his number asking for urgent UPI payments. The fraudsters managed to steal around ₹72,000 from many people before the accountant could warn his contacts and get his WhatsApp back.

In another case, a retired government employee in Lucknow, Mr Singh, received an SMS. It said, 'Your SBI Net Banking will be suspended. Update KYC via link.' He panicked. He clicked the link. It led to a perfect replica of the SBI net banking page. He entered his user ID, password and even the OTP when prompted. Moments later, he received an alert: ₹3 lakh had been transferred from his savings account. His life savings, gone! He was devastated.

What Could Have Helped

- Look at the Email Address: Often, fake emails have strange spellings or extra characters. Like 'sbi.support@gmail.com' instead of 'customercare@sbi.co.in' or 'customer.care.icicibank@gmail.com' instead of 'customer.care@icicibank.com'. Always verify the domain name.

- Check the Official Bank Website: Always type your bank's official website address directly into your browser. Never use links from SMS, emails or even search engine ads that look suspicious.
- Check the URL in the Address Bar: Even if you clicked a link by mistake, look at the address bar. Is it exactly your bank's website? Or does it have strange spellings or extra words? For example, 'sbi-online.com' is fake, 'onlinesbi.com' is real. You should know which are real websites of your bank.
- Never Click Unknown Links: Banks or telecom companies will never ask you to update KYC details through a link in an SMS or email. They will ask you to visit a branch or use their official app. The URL of fake websites will look different from the real website.
- Directly Verify: If you get such a message, don't panic. Call your bank's official customer care number (the one listed on their official website or your bank passbook) and ask them directly.
- Be Sceptical of Urgency: Scammers often use phrases like 'URGENT', 'LAST CHANCE', or 'ACCOUNT BLOCKED' to create fear and bypass your rational thinking. This is a red flag.

THE 'STUCK PARCEL' LIE

You just got a message about a parcel you never ordered! The SMS or email says your parcel is 'stuck at customs' and you need to pay a small fee by clicking a link. If you click, they either take your money directly or get your bank details.

In October 2023, a homemaker, Mrs Devi, got a message. It said, 'Your international parcel is held. Click to pay customs duty.' She wasn't expecting a parcel, but the message looked official, mentioning 'Indian Customs'. She clicked the link and it took her to a fake payment gateway. She entered her debit card details to pay the ₹800 'duty'. A few minutes later, she got an alert: ₹40,000 had been debited from her account. It was shocking! Fake websites can change anything behind the scenes. She tried to make a small payment of ₹800 but lost ₹40,000.

What Could Have Helped

- Verify If You're Expecting a Parcel: If you're not expecting anything, then it's most likely a scam.
- Check Tracking on Official Websites: If you are expecting a parcel, use the official tracking number on the courier company's website (i.e., India Post, Blue Dart, FedEx, DHL). Don't click links in suspicious messages.
- Customs Never Ask for Online Payments Via Links: Customs procedures are usually more formal. They don't typically ask for payments through random links in SMS or emails.

YOUR ACCOUNT, THEIR CONTROL

You log in to your email, or your online shopping account or your bank account. But it says 'incorrect password'. You try again. Still 'incorrect.' Then you realise—someone else has taken over your account! This is 'account take over fraud'.

This happens when fraudsters get your login details for one of your online accounts. They often do this using phishing links. They may also get passwords from other sites' data breaches. Most people use a common password across websites, and login is mostly via email. Once they have access, they can change your password, lock you out and then use your account for their benefit. They might send messages to your friends asking for money, or use your saved payment details. They can also change your delivery address for online shopping, buy things using your saved card details, transfer money from your bank account or even sell your account information to other criminals.

In November 2024, a young professional in Hyderabad, Aisha, got a text message. It said her Instagram account was being logged into from a new device and asked her to click a link to 'verify'. She clicked. The link looked like Instagram's login page. She entered her username and password. The next morning, she couldn't log in. Her friends started calling her, saying they had received messages from her asking for money urgently. Her Instagram account was taken over. It caused her a lot of stress and embarrassment.

In early 2025, a man named Ramesh from Mumbai, who loved travelling, clicked on a phishing email that looked like it was from his airline's loyalty programme. It asked him to log in to check his points. He entered his details, and nothing seemed to happen. The next morning, he received a confirmation email for a premium international flight to Dubai that he had never booked. His account had been hijacked, his points worth around ₹50,000 had been wiped out and a stranger was flying on his dime. The frustration and helplessness he felt was immense.

Mr Singh, a retired teacher in Pune, found himself in a fix on 20 April 2024. He got an SMS alert from his bank about a large transfer of ₹50,000. He immediately tried to log into his net banking account, but his password wasn't working. Someone had logged in, changed his password and transferred money to an unknown account. His identity was compromised. It was later found that his email ID and password were part of a data breach from an old website he used. The fraudsters used this information to access his bank account.

What Could Have Helped

- Don't Click Links for Account Verification: If you get such a message, go directly to the app or website and check your account there. Don't use the link.
- Verify Website URLS Carefully: Most fake website URLs will not look genuine. Verify carefully if you click on a link. It takes little extra effort to check this on mobile phones.
- Enable Two-Factor Authentication (2FA): This is a must-do! It means even if they have your password, they need another code (usually sent to your phone) to log in. Most online services offer this. Use it!
- Use Strong, Unique Passwords: Don't use the same password for all your accounts. Once someone knows your password, the same password can be used for another website. Login is often via email.
- Regularly Check Account Activity: Keep an eye on your account activity for any suspicious logins or transactions. Read email and SMS alerts carefully.

- Be Aware: If you hear about a data breach on a website you use, change your password for that site and any other site where you used the same password.

THE 'LOCKED COMPUTER' NIGHTMARE

This is a really nasty scam. You might get an email with an attachment that looks harmless—maybe a resume, or an invoice. Or a link in an email. If you click the link or open the attachment, a special kind of malicious software (malware) enters your computer. It locks all your files. You can't open your photos, your documents, nothing! Then, the fraudsters ask for money, usually in cryptocurrency, to unlock your files. It's like they've kidnapped your data! And then a message pops up saying, 'Pay us money, or your files will be gone forever.' This is 'ransomware'.

In April 2023, a small business owner, Mr Kapoor, received such an email. It seemed to be from a potential client, with a 'quotation' attached. He opened it and within minutes, his computer screen went dark, and a message appeared: 'All your files are encrypted. Pay 0.1 Bitcoin to decrypt them.' Mr Kapoor's entire business data, his customer lists, his accounts—all were locked. He had to pay about ₹2.5 lakh (the value of 0.1 Bitcoin at that time) because he couldn't afford to lose his data. Many businesses have faced this scam.

A small business owner, Ms Priya, who runs a boutique in Jaipur, faced this nightmare on 5 November 2022. One morning, when she tried to open her business accounting software, she saw that it was all scrambled. A message appeared on the screen demanding $500 (around ₹40,000) in Bitcoin to unlock her files. All her customer data, invoices and designs had become inaccessible. She was desperate, so she paid the ransom, hoping to get her data back. Thankfully, she got it back, but it was a terrifying experience and a huge financial hit.

What Could Have Helped

- Be Careful with Email Attachments: If you don't know the sender, or if the email looks suspicious, don't open any attachments.
- Use Antivirus Software: A good, updated antivirus program can often detect and stop ransomware.
- Back Up Your Data Regularly: This is super important! Keep copies of your important files on an external hard drive or a cloud service like Google Drive, OneDrive, etc. Even if your computer gets locked, your data will be safe.
- Beware of Phishing: Think before you click any links, even those in seemingly legitimate emails.
- Always Be Careful What You Click On: While it is not the core of the scam, ransomware often gets in through phishing emails with bad links or attachments.

SOMEONE ELSE'S VICTIM

Identity theft is when someone steals your personal information—your name, address, Aadhaar number, PAN details, date of birth, etc., to open bank accounts in your name, take loans or even commit crimes. Clicking on malicious links that ask for your personal details is a common way in which they get this information.

In September 2024, a young woman named Pooja who worked in Gurgaon, clicked on a link that promised a 'free government scheme' application. It asked for her Aadhaar number, PAN and a scanned copy of her signature. She provided everything, hoping to get some benefits. A few months later, she started getting calls from banks about overdue loans she never applied for! Someone had stolen her identity to get loans worth ₹5 lakh in her name. It took her months to prove that she wasn't the one who took the loans.

What Could Have Helped

- Be Careful about Sharing Personal Documents Online: Aadhaar, PAN and your signature should only be shared with trusted, official sources.
- Check Your Credit Score Regularly: Websites like CIBIL let you check your credit score and report. This can help you detect if someone has taken a loan in your name.
- Check Income Tax AIS Regularly: Income tax tracks all bank accounts and transactions that are made using your PAN number.

THE 'GHOST SHOPPER'

This happens when fraudsters get your credit card or debit card details, often through phishing links that lead to fake shopping websites. Or they use key-loggers (software that records what you type) installed by a malicious link. Once they have your card details, they use them to buy things online. Sometimes they even buy things in your name to be delivered to a different address.

In December 2023, Mr Roy, a retired teacher in Kolkata, received an SMS saying his Amazon Prime membership was expiring, and to click a link to renew. He clicked on it, and the page that opened looked exactly like Amazon Prime. He entered his credit card details on the page. A few days later, he got alerts for several large online purchases for electronics he never ordered, totalling ₹75,000! His card details had been stolen through the fake Amazon link.

What Could Have Helped

- Always Go Directly to the Shopping Website: Don't use links from emails, SMS or WhatsApp, especially for things like membership renewals.
- Monitor Your Bank Statements: Check your bank and credit card statements regularly. If you see any transactions you don't recognise, report them immediately.
- Set Up Transaction Alerts: Most banks offer SMS alerts for every transaction. This is a great way to know immediately if something is wrong.

While these stories might sound scary, my intention is to empower you. Knowledge is your biggest weapon and by understanding these simple tricks, you can protect yourselves and your families. Remember, if something feels off, or too good to be true, it probably is. Always verify, always be suspicious and always think before you click! Your awareness is the first step to outsmarting scammers.

CHAPTER FOUR

When Apps Lie

Sometimes things online look and feel very real, but they are often a lie. Scammers are incredibly clever; they make fake websites and apps that look just like existing, known ones, or they create new sites that appear genuine. They show you exactly what you want to see—like promises of huge profits on investments—to trick you into giving away your hard-earned money. Which is why we need to be vigilant, always! Let me share some stories to help you understand.

TOO GOOD TO BE TRUE

Imagine you're looking for a new smartphone, a fancy one, at a great discount. You find a website that looks exactly like a popular e-commerce site, maybe like Flipkart or Amazon. The logo is there, the colours are right, even the product descriptions look genuine. You think, 'Wow, what a deal!' You immediately rush to add the smartphone to your cart and begin the checkout process. You are asked to share your payment details to confirm the purchase. Unknowingly, you've just handed your sensitive information directly to criminals.

In early 2024, a young college student, Rohan from Bengaluru, saw an online ad for an iPhone 15 Pro Max at an unbelievable price, nearly half off, on a website that seemed just like that of a well-known online retailer. He was so excited, that he quickly ordered it for ₹75,000 online. He waited and waited, but the phone never came, and the website disappeared too. He realised that he had been duped. His dreams of a new phone were shattered, and his savings gone.

What Could Have Helped

- Check the URL: Always look at the website address carefully. Scammers often use slightly different spellings, like 'amaz0n.in' instead of 'amazon.in'. See that zero '0' which looks like an 'O'. That's a red flag!
- Too Good to Be True: If a deal seems too good to be true, it probably is. No genuine seller will offer expensive products at a drastic discount.
- Cash on Delivery (COD): If possible, choose COD for new websites, especially if you are unsure. This way, you pay only after you receive the product and verify it.
- Research: A quick Google search for reviews of the website can revealed that it is fake.

THE LURE OF QUICK RICHES

Online scammers play on our desire to grow money quickly. They create fancy-looking websites or mobile apps that promise unbelievable returns on your investments. They might even show you fake dashboards where your money seems to be growing fast.

One such incident happened in May 2025, where over 200 people from Karnataka, including Bengaluru, Mangaluru and Hubballi, lost nearly ₹2 crore to a fraudulent app called 'Trump Hotel Rental'. The scammers used AI-generated videos and images of Donald Trump to make the app look legitimate. They promised very high returns, in some cases, over 100 per cent profit in a short period. People invested lakhs, hoping to become rich. One lawyer lost around ₹6 lakh. Initially, they were paid small amounts to build trust, but when they tried to withdraw larger sums, the app vanished. Imagine the despair and fear.

In early June 2025, a twenty-six-year-old man from Hyderabad lost over ₹10 lakh in an investment scam. He got a WhatsApp message offering a part-time job, promising ₹40,000–50,000 per month for just two to three hours of work in a week. He was added to a Telegram group and asked to register on a fake website that looked like a real estate firm's web page, and was even given tasks to 'promote' fictional properties. Initially, he saw a fake ₹10,000 bonus on the app and was allowed to withdraw ₹500 as bait. His balance on the app showed ₹1.72 lakh at one point! But when he was asked to invest all of it for 'greater profits', he got suspicious. By then, he had already lost his hard-earned money which amounted to ₹10,19,781.

In another case, Priya, a young professional in Mumbai, was looking for ways to grow her savings. She saw an ad on social media which promised huge returns on a new 'international trading platform'. It looked very fancy, with charts and live updates, just like those on real trading apps. She downloaded the app from a link they sent her. Priya started with a small investment, ₹10,000. She saw her money growing quickly on the app, which excited her. She invested more, ₹1 lakh, then ₹2 lakh. She even got a small 'profit' withdrawal to build her trust. By November 2022, she had put in a total of ₹5 lakh.

But when she tried to withdraw a larger amount, problems began. The app started to show error messages, 'customer support' stopped replying, and soon, the app itself disappeared. Priya lost all her money. It was a fake app, designed just to show fake profits and steal money.

Another sad case is from Bengaluru, around March 2025. A defence employee was looking for a part-time job for his wife, and he put his contact details online in hopes of receiving opportunities. Soon, he got added to a Telegram group. The administrator, who called herself 'Muskan Aggarwal', said she was an HR manager from an e-commerce company. She offered him a remote job promoting products by adding them to an online shopping cart.

He decided to do the job himself and started with small tasks, like paying ₹150, and he even got ₹1,650 back. He thought, 'Wow, this is working!' Then, the tasks got bigger, asking for ₹3,000, then ₹7,000. He was even pushed to invest in cryptocurrency, under the instruction that he has to pay ₹38,000 within sixty seconds or he would lose everything. He felt pressured, and he transferred the money. The other group members kept showing fake screenshots of earnings. By the end, he had transferred a total of ₹5 lakh. Only when they asked for another ₹1.9 lakh just to withdraw money from the website did he realise it was a big scam.

What Could Have Helped

- Beware of High Returns: If an investment promises abnormally high returns in a short time, it's almost always a scam. Real investments have risks and more realistic returns.
- Verify the Company: Always research the company you choose to invest in. Check their registration, their physical address and read independent reviews.
- No Pressure: Genuine investment firms will never pressure you to invest immediately. They will give you time to think and understand.
- Official Sources: Only download apps from official app stores like Google Play Store or Apple App Store. Never click on links sent via SMS or WhatsApp to download apps.
- Always Do Your Research: Be sure to do your own research about any investment platform. Check if it's registered with the Securities and Exchange Board of India (SEBI).

THE ATTRACTION OF COINS

Cryptocurrency is exciting for many people. Scammers take advantage of this by creating fake crypto exchanges or investment platforms. They promise you huge returns on your crypto investments, but these are just an illusion. Your money disappears into their pockets; they make you believe you're buying 'digital gold', but it's only digital dust.

In early 2025, many people in Bhopal and surrounding districts lost their life savings to various fake cryptocurrency investment apps. These apps would initially show impressive, but fake, profits on a dashboard and even allow small withdrawals to build trust. One such case involved a crypto app where over 250 victims came forward, losing crores of rupees. The money was siphoned off through complex layers of crypto wallets, making it almost impossible to trace. Imagine the heartache of watching your life savings vanish in the blink of an eye.

Deepak from Hyderabad was very keen on being involved with cryptocurrencies as he heard stories of people becoming rich quickly. One day, he joined a WhatsApp group about crypto trading. The group admin told him about a 'new, upcoming cryptocurrency' that would explode in value. They shared a link to a 'crypto exchange' website and asked him to download their app.

Deepak invested ₹75,000. On the app, he could see his 'investment' growing. The numbers were impressive. He even got some messages showing 'successful trades'. He began to dream of buying a new car. But when he tried to sell his 'coins' or withdraw money, he simply couldn't. The platform kept asking for more money for 'taxes' or 'withdrawal fees'. Deepak realised something was wrong when the platform suddenly became unreachable in January 2023. He had invested in a fake currency on a fake platform, and his ₹75,000 was gone.

What Could Have Helped

- Be Wary of Social Media Platforms: Be very careful with crypto investments promoted in WhatsApp groups or Telegram channels. Many of these are run by fraudsters.

- Research Exchanges: Only use well-known, regulated cryptocurrency exchanges. Do thorough research before putting your money into any platform.
- Don't Trust Secretive Ventures: Never invest in cryptocurrencies you've never heard of, especially if they are promoted as exclusive or secret.
- No Guaranteed Returns: No legitimate crypto investment guarantees high returns as the crypto market is very volatile.
- Be Wary of 'Pump and Dump': Scammers often create 'pump and dump' schemes where they inflate the price of a fake crypto, lure investors, and then sell off, leaving others with worthless assets.
- Too Good to Be True: If someone says you'll double your money in days, it's usually a scam.
- Consult Experts: If you are new to crypto, consult financial advisers or experts from reputable institutions before investing.

ONLINE GAMBLING SCAMS

These scams promote illegal online gambling platforms, often promising huge, unrealistic wins as bait. They exploit people's desire for quick money, which can lead them to severe financial loss and addiction. These scammers often use catchy advertisements and even celebrity endorsements to lure you in. They promise you a jackpot, but it's often just a blackhole where your money gets sucked.

In late 2024, a businessman from Navi Mumbai lost a staggering ₹2.74 crore to an online gaming app fraud. He was lured with fake promises of prizes and high returns. He was told to transfer money to multiple bank accounts, and was under the impression that he was participating in various prize-winning games. He managed to recover ₹50 lakh, but the rest was beyond reach. The app just disappeared. This shows how quickly online gambling can become a trap, not just for individuals but for businesses too.

In a truly heartbreaking incident, a seventeen-year-old boy from Siliguri reportedly took his own life after losing nearly ₹2.5 lakh from his father's bank account to an online gaming scam. He was an eleventh-grade student, lured by the promise of easy money. Beyond financial loss, these scams have a severe human cost too.

What Could Have Helped

- Legal and Regulated Platforms: Only engage with online gaming or betting platforms that are legal and regulated in India.
- Unrealistic Promises: Be highly suspicious of any platform promising guaranteed wins or extremely high returns in gambling. Gambling inherently involves risk.
- Check Reviews: Research the platform thoroughly. Look for genuine reviews, not just the ones promoted by the platform itself.
- Seek Help for Addiction: If you or someone you know is struggling with a gambling addiction, please seek professional help. There are many organisations in India that can provide support.

These stories detail a few examples, but the world of cybercrime is always evolving. Remember, knowledge is your sharpest tool so stay alert. Your hard-earned money and peace of mind are precious, and it's only right to protect them.

CHAPTER FIVE

Video Traps

Video calls are very popular these days, we use them to talk to family who live far away or even for work meetings. They help us feel close to people, no matter how far apart we are.

But because video calls are so commonly in use, they've also created a new problem: video call scams. And in India, more and more people are falling prey to them. These scammers aren't just making random calls, they use smarter tricks. They might pretend to be CBI officers, bank employees or close family members, and sometimes they even use new technology like AI and deepfakes to look and sound very real. They trick us by playing on our trust or fear. They create urgent situations to make us share private information or send them money.

This chapter will explain to you the different kinds of video call scams and how they work. Most importantly, it will give you simple tips to protect yourself and your family from these scams.

'DIGITAL ARREST'

The key in this scam is that it uses fear to trap you. Imagine getting a video call, and the person on the other end is wearing a police uniform or looks like a government officer. They tell you that you've done something wrong, like money laundering or drug trafficking, and you are under 'digital arrest'. They say you can't talk to anyone and must follow their instructions. They scare you. And then they ask you to transfer money to 'clear your name'. It's a terrifying experience, and they use pure fear to manipulate you. They might even show you a fake police station in the background. People lose money in crores to this, it is, unfortunately, a very serious scam.

A professor in Nerul fell victim to this 'digital arrest' fraud, and lost ₹1.81 crore. The method of the scam was similar: a call claiming Aadhaar misuse, followed by threats of legal action and a demand for immediate money transfer. These incidents show that scammers target everyone, from senior citizens to educated professionals.

Mr Joshi, a retired school principal in Ahmedabad, received a call in late 2023. The caller claimed to be from the Mumbai Police. 'Mr Joshi, there's a parcel in your name that is linked to drug trafficking and money laundering. You are under digital arrest!' Mr Joshi was terrified. He had never done anything illegal. The caller then connected him to another person, who pretended to be a CBI officer, making the situation appear even more real. They demanded ₹5 lakh to 'clear his name' and warned him not to tell anyone. Mr Joshi, worried about his reputation and freedom, transferred ₹3 lakh from his savings to clear his name.

Dr Awasthi, a respected surgeon from Delhi, received a terrifying call in September 2023. The caller claimed to be from the CBI. They said a parcel with illegal drugs was found in his name in Mumbai, and threatened immediate arrest. They then put him on a video call with a person in a police uniform (which was fake), and told him to transfer all his money to a 'safe government account' for 'verification' and to 'prove his innocence'. Dr Awasthi, panicked and wanting to protect his reputation, transferred ₹8 lakh from his savings. Later, he realised it was a scam when the callers became unreachable. The mental stress for him was immense.

Ms Sharma, a software engineer from Hyderabad, got another such call in November 2023. The caller claimed to be from the Narcotics Control Bureau, and said that a suspicious parcel linked with her Aadhar card details had been intercepted. It contained illegal substances. They pressured her, saying that her career would be ruined if she did not address this. They told her to stay on the call and not tell anyone. Then they proceeded to demand ₹50,000 for 'evidence clearance'. Ms Sharma, who was terrified, transferred the requested amount through UPI, but they kept demanding more. Luckily, her brother overheard her panicked conversation and intervened. She was saved from losing more than ₹50,000.

Mrs Verma, who ran a small boutique in Mumbai, received a chilling call in January 2024. The caller, claiming to be from the Reserve Bank of India (RBI), said that her bank account was involved in a money laundering case. They said that her accounts would be frozen and she would face severe legal action. They created a sense of urgency, and told her to transfer ₹3 lakh to a 'temporary holding account' to 'clean' her funds. Panicked and fearful that her business would be ruined, she transferred the amount. She grew suspicious when they kept demanding more money, and realised it was a scam when she called her bank. She lost ₹3 lakh.

What Could Have Helped

- Remember This: No government official or police officer will ever put you under 'digital arrest' or ask you to transfer money over a video call. As of the publication of this book, 'digital arrest' is not a legal process.
- Always Verify: If someone claims to be from a government agency, always, always verify their identity by calling the official helpline of that department. Government agencies use proper, official channels for communication, not random video calls on WhatsApp or any other app for serious legal matters.
- Don't Panic: Scammers use fear to make you rush. Sometimes they will show you fake arrest warrants and other documents. Take a deep breath, and consult a trusted family member or friend.
- Always Report: Report such calls immediately to the National Cybercrime Reporting Portal (*www.cybercrime.gov.in*) or call helpline number 1930.
- Be Careful with Personal Details: Never share your OTP, banking details or personal information with anyone who calls you, even if they claim to be from a bank or the police.
- Never Be Pressurised: If they pressure you to make an immediate payment, that's a huge red flag. Always take your time to verify.

- Beware of Fishy Video Calls: If you get a suspicious video call, disconnect immediately. Block the number. Inform your family and report it to the cybercrime helpline number (1930) or the cybercrime portal.

NO FRIENDLY FACES

Imagine you're relaxing at home, and suddenly you get a video call from someone you know; maybe a friend, a relative or even someone official. But wait! These video calls can be extremely dangerous. Scammers use them to create trust and then cheat you. Let me explain with some stories.

Around early 2024, Sarla, a lady from Delhi, got a video call on WhatsApp. It was her grandson, Rohan! He looked a bit hazy on the video, but it was him, no doubt. Rohan sounded panicked. He said he had an accident, needed ₹50,000 urgently for treatment and couldn't explain much. Sarla's heart sank. She immediately sent the money through UPI. Later, she called her daughter to check on Rohan. Guess what? Rohan was perfectly fine, at his coaching classes! Sarla had lost ₹50,000 to a scammer who had somehow managed to mimic her grandson's face and voice using technological tricks.

In another case, Ravi, a young graduate from Bengaluru, was super excited when he got a video call for a job interview from a big IT company. The interviewer seemed very professional. He asked Ravi to download a special app for the interview and then to pay a 'refundable security deposit' of ₹15,000. Ravi, dreaming of his new job, paid up. After the call, the number became unreachable, and the company email turned out to be fake. Ravi realised that he had been duped. This kind of scam is common, often for fake part-time or work-from-home jobs.

What Could Have Helped

- Suspect Urgent Money Requests: Always be suspicious if someone asks for money urgently on a video call, even if they look familiar.
- Blurry Video is a Red Flag: If a video call looks blurry or the person's movements seem a bit odd, it could be a trick.
- Call Back on Old Number: The best thing to do is to disconnect and then call that person back on their *known* number to verify. A quick voice call can save you a lot!
- Never Pay for a Job: Real companies never ask for money for job interviews or security deposits.
- Verify Official Website and Email: Always verify the company's official website and contact details. Look for red flags like generic email IDs (Gmail, Hotmail) instead of company-specific ones.
- Don't Download Unknown Apps: If they ask you to download any unknown app, be very careful. It might be malware to steal your data.

SEXTORTION

This is a very nasty scam that preys on your privacy and fear of shame. Scammers connect with you, often through dating apps or social media apps including WhatsApp, and urgently push for a video call, asking you to do something intimate or show yourself nude. Sometimes you may just be on video doing nothing, but the scammer will do something embarrassing. They record it or take screenshots when your camera is on, and then the blackmail begins.

A seventy-three-year-old doctor in Hisar fell victim to a sextortion scam, losing a staggering ₹1.3 crore within just two weeks in August 2024. He received a video call from an unknown woman on WhatsApp. After a nude video call, he began receiving threats, with one individual posing as a CBI inspector. Fearing public humiliation and legal repercussions, the doctor transferred the large sum in instalments. He only realised that he had been scammed after confiding in a friend, who advised him to approach the police.

A sixty-year-old retired man from Hyderabad lost ₹1.6 lakh in an online sextortion scam in May 2025. He received a WhatsApp voice call from an unknown woman. She quickly switched to a video call and started removing her clothes, asking him to do the same. As soon as he did, the call disconnected. Moments later, he got a call from the same number, this time from a man who had his nude video. The blackmailer threatened to share it on social media. Terrified, the man who was caught on video made multiple payments, but the demands didn't stop. Finally, he reached out to the police.

In February 2024, a twenty-three-year-old man from Bengaluru lost ₹44,000 in just two hours. He met a woman on a dating app, and she quickly got his Telegram ID. She coaxed him into a video call, recorded it, morphed it into obscene content and then threatened to send it to his friends unless he paid her an amount. He made the payment, but then realised that it was a scam.

Mr Desai, a businessman from Ahmedabad, received a video call from an unknown number late one night in March 2024. He answered it. On the other end, a naked person appeared briefly before the call disconnected. Soon after, he received a message with a screenshot of his own face from the call, alongside the naked person. The scammer demanded ₹1 lakh. They threatened to send it to his business contacts. Mr Desai was horrified; he paid the money but the demands continued. He lost ₹2.5 lakh before his son noticed his distress and convinced him to confess.

In December 2023, Sonia, a college student from Pune, received a message from an unknown number. It was a picture of her. The message said, 'We have your private photos. Pay ₹30,000 or we will post them everywhere.' Sonia was shocked and scared. She had never shared such photos. The scammer had apparently found some of her old, slightly revealing photos from her social media, edited them and began threatening her. She quickly paid the money out of fear. But they kept demanding more. She lost ₹60,000 before her friend advised her to report it. The emotional toll was immense.

What Could Have Helped

- Be Cautious Meeting People Online: Be very careful about connecting with people online and moving to a private video call quickly. Block and report any suspicious profiles or those that force you immediately for intimate chats.
- Never Share Intimate Videos: Never, ever engage in nude or intimate video calls with strangers, or even people you've just met online. You don't know the person on

the other side. The best thing is to never switch on your camera in these calls.

- Limit Social Media Sharing: Be very careful about what you share on social media. Scammers often use your public photos against your will.
- Do Not Pay the Blackmailer: If you become a victim, do not pay the blackmailer. They will keep demanding more money. Report it to cybercrime police at the earliest.
- Always Report: Even if you have made a mistake, remember that you are the victim. Seek help from trusted friends, family or the police. Shame should not stop you from reporting a crime.

TECHNOLOGY'S LIES

This is the newest, most dangerous trick, and it's driven by technology. Deepfakes use Artificial Intelligence (AI) to create fake videos or audios that look and sound exactly like a real person. Imagine your child calling you, but it's not really her. Or someone who sounds just like your boss urgently asking you for money. This technology makes it very hard to tell what's real and what's fake.

In late 2024, P.S. Radhakrishnan, a seventy-three-year-old retired government employee in Kozhikode, Kerala, lost ₹40,000 to an AI-generated deepfake video. The scammer blended voice and video manipulation to create a convincing emergency scenario. It looked and sounded so real that he didn't question it and lost his money.

Lakshmi Chand Chawla, a senior citizen in Delhi, lost ₹50,000 in October 2024 to a voice-cloning scam. He received a WhatsApp message saying his cousin's son had been kidnapped. To make it believable, the criminals played an AI-cloned voice recording of the child begging for help. Panicked, Chawla transferred the money, and only later did he find out, the child was safe all along.

What Could Have Helped

- Be Mindful While Sharing Videos: Scammers can harvest voice samples from your social media videos or even a 'wrong number' call. Be mindful of what you share online.
- Look for Deepfake Inconsistencies: Deepfakes can make faces look blurry, or the lip movements might not match the spoken words perfectly. Sometimes the voice might sound a bit robotic or flat. Look out for these inconsistencies.
- Suspect Unknown Urgent Calls: If you get a video call from an unknown number, be highly suspicious. Especially if it is an urgent request for money from a person who claims to be someone you know.
- Verify via Second Channel: Verify through another channel. For example, if a call from your child seems like a deepfake, call them back on their known number or text them to confirm. A simple 'Are you really calling me?' can save you.

These scammers are getting smarter every day, using new technology to trick us. But we, too, can be smarter. We should be aware, be cautious and always verify. Our money, our peace of mind and our privacy are precious.

CHAPTER SIX

The 'Call' of Deceit

Cybercrime is like a new disease, spreading fast. And it affects everyone, even good, honest people. These scammers are very clever. But we can be smarter! Your phone 'rings'. You pick it up. A friendly voice, or sometimes a very official one, is on the other side. They sound like they want to help. Or maybe they have good news. But often, it's a trap. Let's see how.

SCREEN MIRRORING

Sometimes we trust too easily, and these fraudsters play on that. In early 2023, Mr Sharma from Delhi got a call. The caller claimed to be from Mr Sharma's bank. 'Sir, your account will be blocked if you don't update your KYC,' the caller said. Mr Sharma, believing him, got worried. The caller asked him to download an app, specifically an app called 'AnyDesk', saying it was to verify his details. Mr Sharma, not knowing much about these things, downloaded the app. The moment he installed it, the scammer could see everything on his phone. Everything! His bank balance, his UPI apps, his personal details. In a few minutes, ₹75,000 was gone from his account, just like that. Mr Sharma was heartbroken. He had been saving that money for his daughter's education.

In another case, Ramesh from Bengaluru got a message about a great job. He was thrilled. It said he just needed to pay a small fee to apply. When he tried to pay online, the payment failed, and soon, a 'customer care' person called him. This person sounded very helpful. 'Sir,' the caller said, 'there's a small technical issue. Please download the "AnyDesk" app. I will guide you.'

Ramesh, trusting the caller, downloaded AnyDesk. He didn't know it was a screen-mirroring app. It lets someone else see and control your phone remotely. As Ramesh opened his banking app, the fraudster was watching everything. Ramesh thought he was making a small payment, but the fraudster quickly transferred ₹50,000 from his account. Ramesh was shocked! This happened in early 2023.

What Could Have Helped

- Never Download Unsolicited Apps: Never download an app if someone tells you to, especially if they tell you over a call. Banks or any official body will never ask you to download an app to 'fix' your account. AnyDesk, TeamViewer, Quick Viewer—these types of apps are mirroring apps and are used by remote persons to see and control your device from far away.
- Banks Don't Use Screen-sharing: No genuine bank or company asks you to download screen-sharing apps like

AnyDesk or TeamViewer. They have their own secure ways to help.

- Call Your Bank Directly to Verify: Always call your bank directly. Use the number on their official website or on your bank passbook, not the one given by a stranger.

THE 'PROCESSING FEE' TRAP

Imagine someone promises you something big—a fantastic job, a huge loan or even a visa. But first, they say, you need to pay a small fee. This is called an 'advance fee scam'. You pay the fee, hoping for the promised benefit. But the benefit never comes. And your money? It's gone forever. It's a cruel trick that preys on people's hopes.

Ms Pooja, a young professional in Pune, needed a quick loan in early 2024. She saw an advertisement on social media for 'Instant Loans, No Documents!', and she called the number. A very sweet-talking person offered her a loan of ₹2 lakh. They didn't have a physical office. All communication was through calls and WhatsApp. They asked her to pay a 'processing fee' of ₹5,000 upfront. Then another ₹3,000 for 'insurance', and so on. Ms Pooja kept paying, hoping to get the loan, paying up to ₹25,000. And guess what? The loan never came. The numbers went silent. She felt utterly cheated.

Who doesn't dream of winning big? But these dreams can turn into nightmares. Mr Ram, a retired government employee in Chennai, got a call in mid-2023. The caller told him that he had won ₹50 lakh in an international lottery! Mr Ram was overjoyed. The caller asked him to pay a 'processing fee' of ₹10,000 to claim his reward. Then a 'tax fee' of ₹20,000. He kept paying, thinking he would get a huge sum back. He ended up paying ₹80,000 in total, and no lottery money ever came. He felt foolish and angry. The money he had paid was meant for his medical expenses.

Priya, a young graduate from Chennai, dreamt of working abroad. In February 2024, she found an agency online promising easy visas to Canada. They asked for an 'initial application fee' of ₹25,000, showing her fake documents. Priya paid the money, excited about her future. Then they asked for another ₹50,000 for 'document verification'. She kept paying, investing her savings. After she paid ₹1.5 lakh, they stopped responding. Her dream was shattered, and her savings were gone. It's heartbreaking to see aspirations exploited in this way.

In December 2023, Mrs Devi, a homemaker from Pune, was overjoyed when she received a message from someone claiming to be an old friend from abroad. The 'friend' said they had sent her an expensive gift. Soon after, she got a call from someone pretending to be from 'customs'. They said her parcel was held, and that she needed to pay a 'customs duty' of ₹30,000 for it to be released. Mrs Devi, excited about the gift, paid the money. Then they asked for more money for 'anti-money laundering clearance'. She kept paying, and lost ₹70,000. The gift never came, and her so-called 'friend' disappeared.

What Could Have Helped

- Never Pay to Get a Prize: You can't win a lottery you didn't enter, it's as simple as that. Never pay money to receive a prize. If you have to pay money to get a prize, it's not a prize; it's a scam.

- Verify Lender's Physical Presence: Legitimate lenders have physical offices. Or at least a proper, verifiable online presence. They don't just operate from phone calls.
- Never Pay Loan Advance Fees: Never pay advance fees for a loan. Reputable banks and financial institutions don't ask for 'processing fees' or 'insurance' upfront before sanctioning a loan. These are usually deducted from the disbursed loan amount. Check their credentials. Are they registered with RBI? A quick search can tell you a lot.
- Use Official Visa Websites: Always use official government websites for visa applications. Be very careful with third-party agencies. Check their accreditation and never pay large upfront sums for 'guaranteed' visas.
- Customs Don't Ask for Direct Payment: Customs officials never call you and ask for direct payments to personal accounts. All customs duties are paid through official government channels.

THE VOICE ISN'T WHAT IT SEEMS

'Vishing' sounds a bit fancy, right? It's simply 'voice phishing'. Scammers phish for your information using a voice call. Mrs Devi from Hyderabad received a call in late 2024. The caller ID even showed her bank's name! The voice sounded very professional. 'Madam, there's been some suspicious activity with your account. We need to verify some details to make it secure again.' Mrs Devi was frightened. She gave her debit card number and the CVV. In a few minutes, ₹50,000 was gone from her account. The scammer had mimicked her bank's number using special software.

What Could Have Helped

- Don't Trust a Caller ID: Caller IDs can be faked. Never trust the caller ID blindly.
- Banks Don't Ask for CVV: Banks never ask for sensitive details like CVV or full card numbers over the phone. They already have this information.
- In Doubt, Hang Up and Call the Bank: If in doubt, hang up immediately. Call your bank yourself using their official number.

THIS NUMBER IS NOT FOR SHARING

This type of fraud is very common. It's like giving someone the key to your bank locker. Just last year, around August 2024, Mrs Singh from Bengaluru got a call where the person on the other end claimed to be from a popular online site. 'Madam, you have won a lottery of ₹10 lakh!' he said. Mrs Singh was thrilled. Then he said, 'To confirm your prize, we need you to share an OTP'. He even sent an OTP. Mrs Singh, in her excitement, read out the OTP number to him. Guess what? It wasn't for a lottery prize. It was for a transaction from her bank account! Before she realised it, and read the complete OTP message, ₹20,000 was debited from her account. She cried a lot. But to no avail.

What Could Have Helped

- Never Share OTP or PIN: Absolutely never share your OTP or PIN with anyone. No bank, no online company, no government agency will ever ask for an OTP or your PIN. It is meant solely for your eyes.
- Read OTP Message Carefully: Always read the message text carefully. Before sharing an OTP, read what the message says. Does it say 'transfer of ₹20,000' or 'login confirmation'? You will know what's happening. Never read out an OTP from a notification as you might miss crucial details.
- Too Good to be True? If it sounds too good to be true, it probably is. Lotteries you didn't enter, prizes you didn't expect—these are often scams.

DON'T JUST CLICK 'PAY'

UPI has made our lives very easy, but scammers have also found a way to misuse it. Mr Gupta, a small shopkeeper in Lucknow, faced the effects of this in late 2023. He was selling an old washing machine online. A buyer called him. 'I'll pay you through UPI,' the buyer said. Then, Mr Gupta received a 'collect request' on his UPI app. It said something like, 'receive payment for washing machine'. The buyer was on the phone, rushing him, saying, 'Just accept it, sir, and then you'll get the money.' Mr Gupta, thinking it was a payment request, clicked 'Accept' and entered his UPI PIN. But instead of receiving money, ₹15,000 was debited from his account! He was entirely confused. The buyer had sent a 'collect request', which means he was asking Mr Gupta to pay him, not the other way around.

What Could Have Helped

- Always Understand UPI Requests: If someone is sending you money, they don't need a 'collect request'. They just transfer it to your UPI ID. You never need to enter your PIN to receive money. You do not have to 'accept' a payment. Money comes to your account automatically.
- Be Wary of 'Requests': If you are receiving money, you should get an SMS that says 'money received', not a request to pay.
- Don't Let Anyone Rush You: Take your time to read and understand any transaction or request before approving it.

PRESS 1 TO LOSE YOUR MONEY

Imagine this: your phone rings, it's an automated voice, just like when you call your bank or telecom company, and it sounds very official. This call is to scare you. The automated voice might tell you that your bank account is frozen, or that your electricity will be cut as you have pending dues. That's what Interactive Voice Response (IVR) scams are all about. These scammers use recorded messages to scare you or trick you into doing something quickly, without thinking.

This is a very common type of fraud, with multiple reports coming in from across India. In early 2025, a Mumbai resident, let's call him Rajesh, gets an automated call. The IVR message says, 'This call is from FedEx. Your parcel has been seized by customs due to illegal drugs found inside. Press 1 to speak to a customs officer.'

Rajesh was shocked. He hadn't sent any such parcel. But the message sounded official. The IVR made it even more authentic. The idea of illegal drugs was scary. He pressed '1'. Then, a person pretending to be a customs officer connected. He spoke very sternly, even threatening Rajesh with arrest and money laundering charges. He said Rajesh needed to transfer a 'security deposit' to a government account to prove his innocence, or his bank accounts would be frozen. He even showed him fake documents and official-looking websites. Under this tremendous pressure, Rajesh ended up transferring ₹7.5 lakh over a few hours. Rajesh realised he was scammed only after the 'officer' stopped responding. It's a truly terrifying experience to be put under such stress.

Here's another example from Bengaluru in July 2023. A sixty-year-old person got a message, supposedly from BESCOM (the electricity board of Bengaluru), saying their bill wasn't paid and that their power would be cut. The message had a phone number for queries. When they called, an IVR system asked them to press certain keys (mostly related to payments). After following the instructions, ₹53,545 was debited from their account. What a sneaky way to trick someone! It's unclear what specific keys were pressed, but they were certainly sufficient to approve the transaction.

What Could Have Helped

- Always Be Wary of Unknown Numbers: Electricity boards or other service providers usually send messages from a recognised sender ID, not a random mobile number.

- Never Share Details or Press Buttons on Unsolicited Calls: If a call/caller asks you to press a button to avoid a service disconnection or to resolve an issue, be extremely cautious. It's often a trap to gain remote access or trick you into sharing sensitive information.

A Few More Common IVR Tricks

- 'Your KYC is Pending': They'll say your bank account or mobile number KYC needs updates and will ask you to press a key to speak to an agent. This agent will then try to get your details which can put you at risk.
- 'You've Won a Lottery!': They'll say you've won a huge prize and need to pay a small 'processing fee' or 'tax' by following IVR instructions. Remember, IVR can be used in any scam.

Understanding IVR Scams

IVR is an automation used by legitimate companies, but unfortunately, scammers also leverage it. These automated IVR calls can appear highly authentic, and scammers use them to dial many people automatically. Only a few people press buttons, and scammers target these individuals, knowing they have fallen for the initial IVR message and can be easily scammed.

It's tough to deal with such scams, and it's normal to feel helpless. But by being informed and vigilant, we can protect ourselves and our hard-earned money.

BOGUS TECH SUPPORT

Sometimes our computers act up, and these fraudsters are all too eager to 'help'. Take the case of Mr Kumar, a software engineer in Noida, who got a pop-up on his laptop in early 2025. It said, 'Your computer is infected! Call this number for technical support.' He called the number. A person with a foreign accent claimed to be from a big software company. He said Mr Kumar's computer had a very serious virus. To fix it, he asked Mr Kumar to give him remote access to his computer and then demanded ₹15,000 for 'repair services'. Mr Kumar paid him, fearing his data would be lost. The 'virus' was fake. The 'tech support' was fake. He lost the money and his peace of mind.

Similarly, Suresh, a small shop owner from Delhi, received an email in January 2024. It looked like it was from his antivirus company. It said, 'Your antivirus subscription has expired. Click here to renew.' Suresh clicked the link. It took him to a page asking for his credit card details to pay ₹5,000. He entered his details. Later, he realised his antivirus was still active, and the email was fake. He lost ₹5,000.

Then there's the story of Mrs Lakshmi, a retired teacher from Chennai, who was using her laptop in August 2023. Suddenly, a big red pop-up appeared. It said, 'Your computer is infected with a dangerous virus! Your bank account is at risk! Call Microsoft Support immediately at 98765XXXXX (scammer's number).' Mrs Lakshmi got scared. She called the number that was shown. The person, speaking in a foreign accent, took remote access to her computer and pretended to 'fix' things. They then said the 'fix' would cost ₹15,000. She paid it through online banking. Later, she realised her computer was fine, and the 'support' was fake. She lost ₹15,000 for nothing.

What Could Have Helped

- Ignore Tech Support Pop-ups: Real tech support companies, like Microsoft or Apple, do not send pop-up messages with phone numbers asking you to call them.
- Never Give Remote Access: Never give anyone you don't trust remote access to your device. It's like giving them control of your entire digital life.
- Use Updated Antivirus Software: Always use reliable antivirus software and update it regularly. Run a good antivirus scan.

THE 'UNDELIVERED PACKAGE' LIE

Ever received a call saying a parcel meant for you is stuck at customs? They say it has something illegal, or it's very expensive. They create urgency and fear, and say you need to pay a 'fine' or 'customs duty' to get it released. But there is no parcel, there are no customs officials. It's just a scammer trying to scare you into paying.

Ms Seema, a student in Bengaluru, got a call in early 2024. The caller claimed to be from an Indian customs officer. 'Your international package has been held because it contains illegal items. You need to pay ₹12,000 to release it, or face legal action.' Ms Seema remembered ordering something from abroad. She panicked. The caller even created a fake tracking ID and website to show her. She paid the money using a link they sent her. The package never arrived. And the customs officials were fake. She lost her precious savings of ₹12,000.

Mrs Singh, a homemaker from Delhi, received a call in September 2023. The caller claimed to be from 'Mumbai customs', and said that a parcel with her name and address had been intercepted. It contained illegal drugs and fake passports. They transferred the call to someone claiming to be a police officer who informed her that she was involved in a serious crime. They told her to stay on the line and not tell anyone. Then they demanded ₹5 lakh to 'settle the case'. Mrs Singh, terrified, transferred ₹3 lakh from her savings. The scammers kept demanding more, and she ultimately lost ₹5 lakh. It was a harrowing experience.

Mr Rao, a retired government official from Hyderabad, received a call in October 2023. The caller claimed to be from a 'courier company', and said a high-value gift from his relative abroad was stuck at customs. They said the package contained a laptop and an expensive watch. They asked him to pay a 'customs duty' of ₹40,000. Mr Rao, excited about the gift, paid the amount to a provided bank account. Afterwards, they asked for another ₹25,000 for 'anti-money laundering clearance', which he also paid. After he paid ₹65,000, the calls stopped, and the 'gift' never arrived.

A young student, Akash from Chennai, received a call in November 2023. The caller claimed to be a 'customs officer', and claimed a package containing gold bars had been seized in his name at the airport. They threatened him with legal action if he didn't pay a 'penalty' of ₹70,000. Akash, scared about legal trouble, arranged the money and transferred it. He lost ₹70,000.

What Could Have Helped

- Customs Clearance is Procedural: Customs officials don't call you to demand bribes. They follow proper procedures.
- Use Official Tracking Website: Check the official tracking website. If you've ordered something, track it on the official courier website, not on some random link.
- Beware Immediate Payment Threats: Be wary of threats. Any call that threatens legal action or consequences if you don't pay immediately, is a red flag.
- Block and Report Scam Calls: If you receive such a call, disconnect immediately, block the number, and report it to the cybercrime helpline (1930) or the cybercrime portal.

CALL FORWARDING SCAM

It was around January 2023. Mrs Sharma, a lady from Delhi, got a call. The caller sounded very official, claiming to be from her mobile company. He told her there was a problem with her network, and she needed to dial a special code to fix it. He said, 'Madam, please dial *401# followed by this number: 98765XXXXX. It's just for a quick network refresh.'

Mrs Sharma, trusting him, quickly dialled the number. She thought she was helping herself. But what she didn't know was that *401# is a code to forward all your calls to another number! So, all her incoming calls, including those important OTP calls from her bank, started going to the scammer's phone.

Within minutes, she got an SMS saying that money was debited from her account. She lost ₹75,000! She was in tears. 'How could this happen?' she was baffled.

What Could Have Helped

- Never Dial Call Forwarding Codes: Your mobile company or bank will never ask you to dial *401# or any similar code. These codes are for call forwarding, and scammers use them to hijack your calls.
- Call Back the Official Number Only: If someone calls claiming to be from your bank or mobile company, always tell them you'll call them back on their official customer care number. Find that number on their official website or on your bill.
- Pause, Think, Avoid Urgency: Scammers often create a sense of urgency; they want you to act quickly without thinking. Always take a moment to pause and think.

MISDIRECTED FROM 'MAPS'

Let's talk about Mr Khan, a busy businessman from Mumbai. One evening in April 2024, he needed to find the customer care number for his bank, XYZ Bank, quickly. He just typed 'XYZ Bank' into Google Maps. He saw a branch, found their number and dialled it.

The person who answered sounded very polite. Mr Khan explained his issue. The scammer then said, 'Sir, for security, we need you to download a small app and share your screen, or give us your UPI PIN to verify.' Mr Khan, thinking it was his bank, shared some details. After all, he was just trying to solve his problem.

Suddenly, he saw ₹50,000 vanish from his account! He realised, too late, that he had called a fake number listed on Google Maps, put there by scammers. It's a very common trick, and it's upsetting to see people lose money this way.

What Could Have Helped

- Use Official Website Numbers: Always, no matter what, get contact numbers from the official website of the bank, company or service you're trying to reach. Don't rely on numbers found directly on Google Maps or through a quick search without verifying the source.
- Don't Share Screen or PINs: Legitimate customer care will never ask you to download remote access apps, share your screen or ask for your UPI PIN, ATM PIN or full card details. These are red flags!
- Check for Fake Map Listings: Sometimes fake listings on Google Maps might have suspicious reviews or very few details. A quick check can sometimes reveal that something is off.

FROM GOOGLE SEARCH

Consider young Ms Priya from Bengaluru. It was around July 2023, and she wanted to return a dress she bought online. She searched on Google for 'Myntra customer care number'. The first few results looked official. She clicked on one, and it took her to a website that looked exactly like Myntra's. She found a number there and dialled it.

The person on the other end pretended to be from Myntra. They asked her to make a small 'refund processing fee' payment through a link they sent, promising the full refund would come after. Priya, just wanting her money back, clicked the link and entered her banking details. She thought, 'It's just a small fee, and I'll get my refund.'

But instead of a refund, ₹20,000 disappeared from her account! She had clicked on a fake website, cleverly designed by scammers to look real, and lost her money.

What Could Have Helped

- Verify the Exact URL: Before clicking on any link from a search result, look closely at the website address (the URL). Does it look exactly like the official one (e.g., myntra.com not myntra-support.in or myntracare.co)? Even a tiny difference can mean that the website is fake.
- Use Official App or URL: For online shopping or banking, it's always safest to use the official app or type the website address directly into your browser. Don't rely solely on search results.
- Never Pay a Refund Fee: Legitimate companies will never ask you to pay a fee to process a refund. If someone asks for money to give you money back, it's a scam.
- Don't Click Suspicious Links: Don't click on links sent via SMS or email, especially if they ask for personal or banking details, unless you are absolutely sure of the sender.

THE CALL MERGE SCAM

This scam is very cunning. They make you believe you are talking to your bank, but it's actually all false. Just a few months ago, around March 2025, Mr Prakash, a small business owner in Delhi, got a call from a person claiming to be from his bank's fraud department. 'Sir, we noticed some suspicious activity on your account. Someone tried to make a big transaction,' the caller said in a serious voice. Mr Prakash got worried. The caller then said, 'To verify this, we will connect you to our OTP verification system. You will receive a call from the verification system, please merge it using conference with this call.'

While Mr Prakash was still on the line with the scammer, his actual bank's automated OTP voice service called him! Yes, a real call from his bank. The scammer had initiated a transaction using Mr Prakash's details. Mr Prakash merged the OTP call with the existing call with the scammer. Automated OTP call read out OTP for transaction, the scammer listened to the OTP and before Mr Prakash could understand what was happening, ₹85,000 was gone from his business account. He was devastated. That money was meant for his business expenses.

What Could Have Helped

- Banks Don't Ask for OTPs: Be wary of calls claiming 'suspicious activity'. While banks might call for verification, they will never ask you for OTP verification.
- Never Merge Bank Calls: If you receive a second call from an unknown number or from your bank, be extra careful. Disconnect the first call immediately. Never merge that call with the ongoing call.

Do you see how tricky they are? They use technology to make you believe something false. But knowing these tricks is your best defence.

These stories are troubling, but they teach us important lessons. The common thread in all these scams is one thing: they call you, they create urgency and then ask for money or sensitive information.

Remember these simple rules

- Banks will never call you to ask for your PIN, OTP, CVV or full card details.
- If someone promises you a prize, a loan or a job, and asks for money upfront—it's a scam.
- Never download any app on someone's instruction.
- Always verify, verify, verify! If in doubt, hang up and call the official number yourself.

Your money is your hard work. Don't let these scammers take it away. Stay smart, stay secure.

CHAPTER SEVEN

The Clever Cons

We've talked a lot about scams that come to your phone, like those pesky links or calls. But did you know, some clever fraudsters work in different ways? They don't always need a tricky link or a convincing call. They find other routes to fool you. It's important to know about these too. Let's dive in.

THE PACKAGE THAT VANISHED

This is called 'Interception Fraud'. The fraudster already has your credit or debit card details. Maybe they got it from a data leak or from a previous hack. Then, they order something expensive online using your card. But here's the trick: before the delivery, they change the shipping address! So, your new phone goes to their address, not yours. You only realise something is wrong when you see a big charge on your bank statement for something you never got.

Let's talk about what happened to Mr Sharma in Delhi. He was checking his bank statement on 10 December 2023. He saw a charge for a new laptop, ₹75,000! But he hadn't ordered any laptop. He called the online store. They said the laptop was delivered to an address in Gurugram, not his home in Delhi. Someone had used his card and changed the delivery address just before it shipped. Poor Mr Sharma was shocked. It took him weeks to get his money back.

What Could Have Helped

- Use Transaction Alerts: Many banks and online stores send SMS or email alerts for every transaction. If Mr Sharma had signed up for these, he might have seen the purchase alert immediately.
- Check Statements Frequently: Don't wait till the end of the month to look at your bank and cards statements. Check them every few days, especially if you shop online a lot.
- Block the Card, Report Quickly: The moment you see a suspicious transaction, call your bank and block your card. Then, inform the online store. The faster you act, the better your chances of getting your money back.

LOAN SCAMS

Have you ever heard of someone getting a loan without even applying for it? Or someone taking out a loan in your name without your knowledge? This is a 'false documentation' or 'forged signature' scam. Here, fraudsters create fake documents—like Aadhaar cards, PAN cards or even salary slips—and forge signatures. Then they use these fake papers to get loans or credit cards in someone else's name.

Think about Mrs Devi from Chennai. She got a call from a bank on 15 March 2024, asking her to repay a loan. But Mrs Devi had never taken a loan from that bank! She was utterly confused. After checking, she found out that someone had used a forged PAN card and a fake electricity bill with her name and address to get a personal loan of ₹2.5 lakh. The fraudster even forged her signature on the loan application. It was a nightmare for her to prove that she had never taken the loan.

What Could Have Helped

- Write Purpose on Copies: Be very careful with your original documents like Aadhaar, PAN and passport. Don't share photocopies or digital images widely. When you give a copy, write 'for XYZ purpose only' across it.
- Regularly Check Your Credit Score: Regularly check your credit score (CIBIL score). If someone takes a loan in your name, it will show up there. You can get a free report once a year.
- Shred Old Documents Properly: Don't just throw away old bank statements or bills. Shred them properly so no one can piece together your information.

SCRATCH CARD SCAMS

Remember those glossy pamphlets you sometimes got in malls and at festive events? They often had a 'scratch card' that said you've won a big prize, like a new car or a huge sum of money. You scratched it, and wow! You've 'won'! But could it be real? Almost always, it was a scam.

They lure you with the scratch card. Then, they call you, congratulating you on your 'win'. But to get your prize, they ask you to pay a 'processing fee' or 'tax' or some other charge. You pay, and pay, and pay. But the prize? It never comes.

Mr Ramesh from Bengaluru received a fancy brochure in August 2023. It had a scratch card. He scratched it, and it said he won ₹10 lakh! He was over the moon. Soon, he got a call from someone claiming to be from a 'lottery department'. They congratulated him and asked him to deposit ₹20,000 as a 'tax' to release the prize money. Mr Ramesh, in his excitement, sent the money. Then they asked for more, for 'clearance' and 'documentation'. He ended up sending ₹80,000 in total. After that, their phone numbers went dead. Mr Ramesh lost his hard-earned money, and the dream of a lottery win.

What Could Have Helped

- Never Pay for Prize Winnings: Remember, if something sounds too good to be true, it probably is. No legitimate lottery or prize scheme will ask you to pay money to receive your winnings. Tax Deducted at Source (TDS) is taken from the prize. You don't ever have to pay anything.
- Call an Alternate Official Number: If you get such a card, check the company's official website. Call their official customer service number, not the one given on the pamphlet.
- Beware Urgency: Scammers often create a sense of urgency. They say, 'Act fast! This offer is only for a limited time!' This is to pressure you into making a quick decision without thinking.

MARKETPLACE SCAMS

There are many online apps like OLX, which we often use them to buy or sell old things or find places to rent. They're very easy to use. But sometimes bad people, like scammers, use these apps to trick us.

If you' re selling your old couch or buying a phone, be careful. A quick deal that looks too good to be true is often just that. This is a very common scam: a scammer will call you, they'll act like a real buyer and agree to your price right away, without any talk about lowering it. Then, they'll say they want to pay you instantly using UPI (like Google Pay, PhonePe, or Paytm).

Ms Priya, an eighteen-year-old student from Bengaluru, put up her 'One Piece' manga books for sale on OLX in June 2025, hoping to earn some pocket money. Soon, a man named 'Ashok Agarwal' contacted her, agreeing to her price of ₹1,500 for the books without any questions. He insisted on a bank transfer and sent her a QR code, claiming it was for 'account verification' and that she'd receive ₹1 upon scanning it. Hesitantly, Priya scanned the code, and indeed, ₹1 was credited to her account. Convinced it was legitimate, she scanned another QR code Ashok sent for the ₹1,500. But instead of receiving money, ₹1,500 were debited from her account. When she panicked, Ashok reassured her it was a 'technical glitch' and sent another QR code for her to scan using her mother's digital payment app. This time, ₹4,500 was deducted. The scammer continued to insist on 'glitches', leading to further debits of ₹19,500 and then another ₹40,500 from her mother's account. In total, Priya and her mother lost ₹90,000. It was only when her father intervened and confronted the caller that they realised the extent of the fraud.

In October 2024, Mehar Kaur Thind and her mother, Rupinder Kaur, from Chandigarh listed a dining table for sale on OLX for ₹20,000. They were contacted by a man identifying himself as 'Mishra', who claimed to be an army officer. He agreed to the price immediately and insisted on an online payment. He then sent Mehar a few QR codes via WhatsApp, instructing her to scan them to receive the payment. Mehar, believing it was a legitimate transaction, scanned the codes, and ₹80,000 were immediately debited from her account. When she questioned this, 'Mishra' claimed it was for 'verification' and that the money would be refunded. He then gained access to Rupinder Kaur's bank accounts under the pretext of completing the transaction and siphoned off another ₹1.99 lakh through multiple transactions. The mother and daughter ended up losing a total of nearly ₹2.8 lakh to the fraudster.

What Could Have Helped

- Never Scan a QR Code or Click a Link to Receive Money: This is the golden rule for UPI transactions. To receive money, you only need to share your UPI ID (your mobile number@UPI, or your VPA).
- Be Wary of Pretenders: Don't trust people claiming to be 'army personnel' or remote buyers/sellers. While genuine cases exist, it is very common for scammers to avoid meeting in person and to build false trust.
- Avoid Advance Payments: For buyers, never pay for an item before physically inspecting it and verifying its authenticity. For sellers, never make any payment (e.g.,

for 'registration', 'delivery' or 'processing') to 'receive' your product's payment.

- Do Not Share OTPs or UPI Pins: Your OTP and UPI PIN are like the keys to your bank account; be very careful with them.
- Meet in Public Places and Inspect Items: For physical goods, always insist on meeting in a public, well-lit location. Carefully inspect the item before completing the transaction.
- Keep Communication on OLX: Scammers often try to move the conversation to WhatsApp or direct calls to avoid OLX's internal monitoring.
- If Scammed, Act Fast: Immediately contact your bank to report the fraudulent transaction. Then, file a complaint on the National Cybercrime Reporting Portal (www.cybercrime.gov.in) or call the national helpline 1930.

IDENTITY THEFT

We have discussed the terrible scam of 'identity theft' previously. It's when someone steals your personal information—your name, address, Aadhaar number, PAN, bank account details—and then uses it to pretend to be you.

While sometimes this information is stolen through digital means, it can also happen offline. For example, if your wallet is stolen, if someone goes through your trash for discarded documents or discarded documents of a company where you have shared personal details. The actual scam is the misuse of your identity.

Ms Fatima, a student in Mumbai, was shocked to receive multiple credit card statements on 1 July 2023, for cards she never applied for. Someone had stolen her identity. They had used her old address, her name and her PAN details (which they likely got from some old discarded document or a data breach) to apply for new credit cards. They then ran up bills of over ₹1.5 lakh on these cards. Ms Fatima had to fight hard to clear her name and prove that she wasn't responsible for these debts.

What Could Have Helped

- Store Documents Safely: Treat your personal documents like gold; store them in a safe place.
- Always Shred Documents: Always shred documents with personal information before throwing them away. Don't just tear them up; use a shredder.
- Limit Social Media Oversharing: Don't overshare personal details on social media. Be mindful of what information you put on public websites.
- Monitor Credit and Statements: Regularly check your credit report and bank statements. Any unusual activity might be a sign of identity theft.
- Beware of Phishing Attempts: Identity theft can also happen through phishing attempts, where scammers try to trick you into giving up your details.

Scammers are always learning and evolving. They share their tricks, find new ways to fool people and constantly adapt. Which is why we need to be just as smart, if not smarter. We need to learn from others' experiences, understand the new scams that are doing the rounds and share that knowledge within our families and communities. That's how we build a strong defence together and keep ourselves safe in this digital world.

CHAPTER EIGHT

Playing Mind Games

Scammers are very cunning. They use a variety of tricks to get your money. They play with your feelings and your mind, make you believe them, create fear, or greed or hope. Let's look at some real-life stories and learn how to protect ourselves.

PLAYING WITH COMPASSION

Many scams don't need fancy computer tricks. Scammers just play with your mind. They are like actors, they create a story to trap you.

This happened to young Rohan from Mumbai in January 2024. He got a WhatsApp message from a number he thought was his friend, Sameer. Sameer's profile picture was there. The message said, 'Hey bro, I'm in a big problem. I need ₹10,000 urgently. My UPI is not working.' Rohan, without thinking, sent the money. Later, he called Sameer to ask about it. Sameer said he never sent any message. Rohan realised his friend's profile picture was used by a scammer. He lost ₹10,000. It's so sad when trust is misused like this.

What Could Have Helped

Always, no matter what, call and confirm with the person if they are asking for money, even if it seems like your friend or family. A quick call can save you a lot of trouble. Their social media accounts could be hacked.

HOPES DASHED

Looking for a job is very tough and scammers know this too. They use your desire for work against you. They offer dream jobs, easy money or work-from-home opportunities, but there's always a catch. You have to pay some fee upfront, or they make you do small tasks and then disappear with your money. It's a sad reality that people's desperation is used against them.

Ravi, a young man from Bengaluru, was desperately looking for a job in July 2023. He saw an online ad for cabin crew positions in a big airline. It promised a high salary. He applied and soon got a call for an 'interview'. The person sounded very professional. They said he was selected! But he needed to pay a 'registration and uniform fee' of ₹15,000. Ravi, thrilled about the job, borrowed money from his family and paid it. Then they asked for ₹20,000 for 'training material'. He paid that too. After he had paid ₹60,000, they stopped answering his calls. The airline confirmed they had no such recruitment. Ravi was devastated.

Legitimate companies never ask for money for job applications, interviews, uniforms or training. Always check the company's official website for job openings and be suspicious of offers that seem too good to be true.

Meena, a college student from Hyderabad, wanted to earn some pocket money. In March 2024, she saw an ad on Telegram for a 'part-time online task job'. It promised ₹1,000–₹5,000 daily. She had to 'like' some videos and get paid. For the first few tasks, she got small amounts. This built her trust. Then they said to get higher commissions, she had to invest small amounts. She invested ₹500, then ₹1,000 and got returns. She became confident. They told her to invest ₹25,000 for a 'VIP task' for a huge return. She did and after that, they blocked her. Meena lost ₹30,000. It's truly upsetting to see young people fall for such cruel tricks.

Be very cautious of easy money schemes, especially those asking for initial investments. If a job promises high returns for simple tasks, it's a red flag. Real part-time jobs don't ask you to invest your own money.

Mr Kumar, a retired government employee from Kolkata, wanted to keep himself busy. In May 2023, he found an online ad for a 'work-from-home data entry job'. They even sent him a contract which looked very official. They asked for a 'security deposit' of ₹5,000, which they promised to refund. Mr Kumar paid it. He did the work, completing many pages of data entry. When he asked for his payment, they said his 'accuracy was low' and he had to pay a 'penalty' of ₹10,000. When he refused, they threatened him with legal action. He realised it was a scam. He lost ₹5,000. It's truly upsetting to see people exploiting the vulnerable.

Be very wary of work-from-home jobs that demand an upfront 'security deposit' or 'registration fee'. Legitimate companies pay you for your work, not the other way around.

Always read the terms and conditions of any job offer very carefully, and check online reviews of the company.

FAKE FRIEND

I want to share a few real-life stories to show how this scam works, how much people have lost and what you can do to stay safe.

Priya, a twenty-eight-year-old teacher from Delhi, loved scrolling through Instagram. In January 2023, she connected with a guy named 'Mark' from Dubai, who seemed charming and sent her photos of his travels. After months of chatting, Mark said he was coming to India to meet her and would bring a gold bracelet as a gift. A week later, Priya got a call from a man claiming to be a customs officer at Delhi's Indira Gandhi International Airport. He said Mark was detained for carrying undeclared $5,000 and demanded ₹75,000 via PhonePe to 'release' him. Panicked, Priya paid the amount, only to find Mark's Instagram account deleted the next day. Her 'friend' was fake, and she lost ₹75,000.

Anil, a thirty-five-year-old shopkeeper from Mumbai, made a friend named 'Sarah' on WhatsApp in August 2024. She claimed to be a businesswoman from London and sent him pictures of her 'luxury lifestyle'. Sarah said she was sending Anil a parcel with a fancy watch and $10,000 as a business investment. Soon, a man claiming to be from Mumbai's Chhatrapati Shivaji Airport customs called Anil, saying the parcel was held for unpaid duties. He demanded ₹1.2 lakh via Google Pay to release it. Anil, excited about the 'investment', paid the amount. When he tried contacting Sarah, her number was off, and he realised the parcel had never existed. He lost ₹1.2 lakh.

Shalini, a thirty-year-old IT professional from Bengaluru, met 'David' on Facebook in March 2024. He claimed to be a doctor from Canada and showered her with compliments. After two months, David said he was flying to Bengaluru to meet her. A day later, Shalini got a call from a 'customs officer' at Kempegowda International Airport, claiming David was detained for carrying undeclared gold worth $8,000. The caller demanded ₹90,000 via Paytm to avoid David's arrest. Shalini, worried for her 'boyfriend', paid immediately. Later, she found out that David's profile was fake, and she had lost ₹90,000.

What Could Have Helped

- Check the Profile: Fake social media accounts often have few posts or no mutual friends. Look for red flags like a recently created account.
- Be Wary of Paying Strangers: Never send money via UPI to unknown numbers. Insist on meeting the 'officer' at the airport or customs office.
- Verify by Tracking: Always ask for a tracking number and check it on the courier's official website, not through WhatsApp links.
- Be Wary of Receiving Gifts: Expensive gifts from online friends are a big red flag.
- Ask for Proof: Insist on a bank transfer with proper documentation, and only after meeting a customs officer, if applicable.

- Be Cautious: Scammers use romance to manipulate. Be cautious of someone you've met online pushing a relationship too fast.

HELPING 'OLD FRIENDS'

This one is really tricky, because it plays with your emotions. Naturally, you will want to help your friends, and scammers know this.

Suresh lived in Delhi. One day, he got a WhatsApp message from his old school friend, 'Rajesh', who lives in the US. The message said, 'Hey Suresh! I'm at Mumbai airport. Customs stopped me. I have some gifts for you. They want some money for customs duty. Can you help me? I'll pay you back instantly.' Suresh felt bad for Rajesh. He remembered Rajesh as a good friend. The scammer even shared a fake customs document, which appeared to be very real. Suresh transferred ₹75,000 to an account. The scammer kept asking for more money, saying there were other charges and that his 'flight' was delayed. Suresh got suspicious. He called Rajesh's real number. And guess what? Rajesh was safe at home in the US! He never travelled. Suresh lost ₹75,000.

Let me tell you about Priya from Bengaluru. Her cousin, Anjali, messaged her in desperation. Anjali was supposedly at Chennai International Airport and said that she was bringing some expensive electronics from Dubai. Customs had held her up and were demanding ₹1.2 lakh. Anjali sounded worried in the messages. She sent a picture of a 'customs officer's ID'. It looked blurry. Priya felt worried for her cousin and sent the money. But then 'Anjali' asked for more, for some 'anti-money laundering' clearance. Priya's husband got suspicious. He called Anjali's parents, who told him that Anjali was at home in Dubai! She wasn't travelling. Priya lost ₹1.2 lakh.

Ramesh from Pune got a message from someone claiming to be his foreign 'friend' from the US. This 'friend' said they were sending some expensive gifts: a laptop and a watch. A few days later, Ramesh got a call. Someone claiming to be from Mumbai customs said the gift was 'stuck', and asked him to pay ₹50,000 for customs duty and a 'release fee'. They gave him bank account details to pay the fees. Ramesh was excited about the gifts, so he paid. Then they asked for another ₹30,000 for 'foreign exchange clearance'. Ramesh paid again. The 'friend' kept messaging, saying 'pay them, it's urgent'. Ramesh lost ₹80,000. He never got any gifts, and his 'friend' vanished.

What Could Have Helped

- Call Your Friend Directly: Always call the person on their earlier known number. Don't just reply to messages from unknown numbers.
- Verify, Verify, Verify: Customs authorities don't ask for money to be sent to personal accounts. This is a big red flag.
- Don't Trust Blurry Photos: Scammers often send low-quality images or fake documents.
- Be Wary of Unexpected Gifts: If you didn't order something, or are not expecting gifts from a known person, be suspicious of communication regarding parcels.
- Check Sender Details: If the 'friend' is messaging from a new number, it can be a huge red flag.

THE 'MISTAKEN TRANSFER' TRAP

Imagine you get a message saying that money has been deposited into your account. Then, someone calls you, sounding frantic, asking you to return the money. They might even send you a fake screenshot of the transfer. But it's a trick! They want you to send money back to them. You might even end up sending more money than you received, or authorising a larger transaction. It's a clever way to play on your honesty.

Mrs Geeta, a homemaker from Bengaluru, received a notification on her phone in February 2024. It showed ₹5,000 were credited to her UPI account. Moments later, she received a call. The person said, 'Oh, I accidentally sent ₹5,000 to your UPI. Can you please send it back?' They even sent a fake screenshot showing a much larger amount that they had supposedly sent. Mrs Geeta, being honest, immediately tried to send back ₹5,000. But the scammer guided her to accept a 'receive' request on her UPI app instead of 'send', and she ended up authorising a debit of ₹10,000 from her account. In this confusion, she lost ₹10,000.

Mr Prakash, a small shop owner from Lucknow, sold an item online in April 2023. He received a message from the 'buyer' saying that they had transferred ₹10,000. They asked him to accept the payment by clicking on a link. Mr Prakash clicked on it, thinking that he will get his money. Instead, ₹10,000 was debited from his account. It was a 'request money' link, and when he approved it, he transferred ₹10,000 to 'buyer'. He ended up losing ₹10,000 instead of receiving money.

A young student, Rohan from Mumbai, received a call in January 2024. The caller claimed to be from a popular digital wallet company and said, 'You have received a cashback offer. To claim it, just enter your UPI PIN.' Rohan, thinking he was receiving money, entered his PIN. Immediately, ₹2,500 were debited from his account. He realised he had been tricked into authorising a payment instead of claiming a cashback. He lost ₹2,500 to this trick.

Suresh from Chennai got a message from PhonePe (fake WhatsApp account) with a screenshot attached. 'Dear customer, a transfer of ₹5,000 has been made to your account by mistake. Please send it back urgently to this number.' The message looked like a genuine transaction alert. Suresh felt it was his duty to return it. So, he quickly sent back ₹5,000 to the number given. But when he checked his bank statement later, the original 'transfer' was never there! The scammer had just sent him a fake screenshot, not actual money. Suresh lost his own ₹5,000.

Deepak from Hyderabad got a call from a woman crying on the phone: 'Oh my God! I sent ₹10,000 to your account by mistake! My mother needs urgent medicine. Please send it back quickly!' Deepak checked his SMS. Yes, there was an alert for ₹10,000. He felt bad for the woman and immediately transferred the money to the account she provided. Only later did he find out that the SMS was fake, designed to look like a real bank alert. He lost ₹10,000.

What Could Have Helped

- Always Check Your Bank Balance First: Don't just trust a message; log in to your bank app and see if the money actually arrived.

- Be Wary of Urgency: Scammers always push you to act fast. Sometimes they even cry. Always take your time to verify the bank account balance first.
- Verify SMS Alerts: Don't trust SMS alerts blindly. Always cross-check with your bank app or by calling your bank's official number.
- Don't Give in to Emotional Pressure: Scammers often use emotional stories to rush you. Don't fall for this, take your time.
- Be Careful with UPI: You only need your UPI PIN to *send* money, not to *receive* it. If someone asks for your PIN to 'receive' money or 'claim cashback', it's a scam.

THE 'WIN BIG' LIE

Everyone dreams of winning big. And scammers know this. They create fake online gambling sites, or apps, promising huge winnings, easy money or assured jackpots. They make you believe you're on the verge of a big win; they might even show you small wins to build your confidence. But in the end, you lose all the money you invested, and there's no real chance of winning anything. It's a sad truth that people often lose their savings to these illusions.

Vikas, a passionate cricket fan from Delhi, was looking for ways to earn extra money. In November 2023, he joined a Telegram group that promised 'fixed cricket matches' with guaranteed wins. The group administrator showed screenshots of past 'winnings'. Vikas was convinced, so he started with a small bet of ₹5,000 and 'won' ₹10,000. This built his trust. He then invested ₹50,000 for a 'big match' with a 'guaranteed' return of ₹5 lakh. After the match, the administrator blocked him and Vikas lost his ₹50,000. He was cheated terribly.

There is no such thing as a 'fixed match' in legitimate sports. Any group or person promising guaranteed wins in gambling is a scammer. Do not trust unsolicited offers for betting or investment schemes, especially on social media platforms. Always remember, gambling is risky, and there are no shortcuts to winning.

Ravi, a young man from Mumbai, got drawn into an online casino advertisement that he saw on Instagram in February 2024. It showed people winning huge amounts. He signed up and deposited ₹10,000. He played some games and even saw his 'balance' increase. When he tried to withdraw his 'winnings' of ₹30,000, the site asked him to pay a 'withdrawal fee' of ₹5,000. He paid it. Then they asked for a 'tax fee' of ₹8,000. He paid that too. This continued, but he never received any money in return. He lost ₹25,000 in total.

Be very cautious of online gambling platforms that are not properly licensed and regulated.

What Could Have Helped

- If It's Too Good to Be True, It Probably Is: Free high-value items often come with hidden catches.
- Research the Contest/Company: Is it a real company? Are there any valid reviews? Look for red flags online.
- Never Pay to Receive a Prize: A real prize is delivered, not bought.
- Check for Legitimate Licenses: If a platform asks for multiple 'fees' to withdraw winnings, it's a red flag.

Legitimate casinos typically deduct fees from your winnings directly.

THE CRYPTO MAZE—'PUMP AND DUMP'

Cryptocurrency is the newest playground for scammers. They use clever tricks to make you invest in fake digital currencies or schemes by creating a lot of hype and making you believe that you'll get rich quickly. This is called 'pump and dump' or 'rug pull'. They 'pump' up the value with fake news, get you to invest and then 'dump' their own holdings, leaving you with worthless digital coins. It's a very modern form of fraud, and it can empty your wallet in a flash.

Raghav, a young investor from Delhi, was keen on cryptocurrencies. In August 2023, he joined a Telegram group promoting a 'new revolutionary crypto coin'. The group members posted fake testimonials and created a lot of hype, saying that the coin would skyrocket. Raghav invested ₹1.5 lakh in the coin. The price went up for a few days, and then suddenly crashed to almost zero. The Telegram group disappeared, and the founders vanished. Raghav realised it was a 'rug pull'—the creators had sold all their coins, leaving everyone else with nothing. He lost ₹1.5 lakh. It's a harsh lesson indeed.

Be extremely cautious of new, unknown cryptocurrencies that are promoted heavily on social media or messaging apps. Always do your own thorough research before investing in anything. Check the project's white paper, team transparency and community sentiment on reputable forums, not just hype groups. Understand that high returns usually come with high risks.

Ms Kavita, a software professional from Bengaluru, was approached on LinkedIn in October 2023 by someone claiming to be a crypto expert. They introduced her to an 'AI-powered crypto investment platform' that promised daily profits of 2–5 per cent. She started with a small investment of ₹20,000 and saw her 'profits' grow on the platform's dashboard. She even made a small withdrawal, which further built her trust. Encouraged by this, she invested ₹5 lakh. When she tried to withdraw a larger amount, the platform suddenly showed an error message, and then disappeared. She lost ₹5 lakh.

Be very sceptical of platforms promising guaranteed high daily returns in cryptocurrency. Such returns are usually unrealistic and unsustainable. Always use reputable, regulated cryptocurrency exchanges. Research the platform thoroughly, check for red flags like vague terms and conditions, lack of transparency and unsolicited approaches.

A group of friends in Pune, including Sameer, got excited about a particular altcoin after a well-known 'crypto influencer' heavily promoted it on YouTube and Twitter in December 2023. The influencer claimed it was the 'next big thing'. Many people invested their money, causing the price to 'pump' up significantly. Sameer invested ₹80,000. After a few days, the influencer stopped talking about the coin. The price of the coin plummeted, and Sameer couldn't sell his holdings without significant losses. It turned out that the influencer had likely been paid to promote the coin and then the original holdings were sold after the price increased (a 'pump and dump' scheme). Sameer lost ₹50,000.

Do not blindly follow 'influencer' advice for crypto investments. Many influencers are paid to promote certain coins, and their advice may not be impartial. Always do your own research and understand the risks involved in volatile assets like cryptocurrencies. Invest only what you can afford to lose.

THE 'DECEPTIVE' FAMILIAR FACE

Scammers cleverly use the logos, names, photos, and often, even the look and feel of well-known companies or brands on their fake websites. They want you to trust them because you recognise the brand; they wear a mask of familiarity to trick you.

Just recently, on 31 May 2025, a woman in Puducherry was duped of a massive ₹5.1 crore in a WhatsApp impersonation scam. The fraudsters used the profile picture of her company's managing director (MD) on WhatsApp and tricked her into transferring funds for an 'urgent business project'. She believed it was her MD's new number and transferred the money from the company's account. The moment she realised it was a scam, it was too late. This shows how even familiar faces can be used for fraud.

What Could Have Helped

- Verify Unexpected Requests: If you receive an unexpected request for money, especially from someone you know, always verify it through another channel (e.g., a phone call to their known number or by meeting them in person). Don't rely solely on the message you receive. These requests often come from an unknown number or account. Scammers may use profile photos of familiar people to build trust.

- Official Communication Channels: Companies usually have official channels for large financial transactions. Be wary of requests coming through informal channels like WhatsApp for significant sums.
- Look for Inconsistencies: Does the language of the person messaging you seem off? Is the tone different from how the person usually communicates? These small details can be red flags.

We've seen how clever these scammers are, they don't just throw random tricks at us; they're really good at playing with our feelings and our thoughts. They make us believe them, creating fear, making us feel greedy for a quick buck or giving us hope for something good. It's really unfortunate when good people, even smart ones, fall for these tricks. But here's the good news: we can always learn. By looking at real stories of how people got scammed, we can learn how to spot red flags, become more aware and know how to protect our families and our hard-earned money.

Part Three

OTHER DANGERS OF ONLINE

CHAPTER NINE

Vulnerable Family Members

In our journey to becoming cyber smart, we have covered a lot of ground. But now, it is time to talk about two important groups in our families: our children and our seniors.

The sad truth is that these two groups are most vulnerable to online dangers. Cyber criminals are very cleverl; they know exactly who to target. And unfortunately, our innocent children and our trusting elders often become easy targets for them. In this chapter, we're going to thoroughly understand why they are at risk, and then, figure out exactly what we can do to protect them.

OUR LITTLE ONES ONLINE

Our children are growing up with mobiles and computers as an integral part of their lives. For them, the internet is like a playground. It's new and exciting. But just like any playground, there can be dangers here too. Which is why we must teach them how to be careful. Let's talk about some common risks they might face.

Online Gaming: Fun or Trouble?

Many children play games online, like Free Fire, PUBG or even simple car racing games. These games are fun and let you connect with friends. But they often have hidden traps.

In-Game Purchases*:* Some games have special features that allow you to buy cool new clothes or special powers for your character. They say, 'Buy this! It's only ₹99!' Or 'Get this special pack for ₹499!' These are called in-game purchases. Our children don't always understand money like we do. They see something shiny, and click 'buy'. And suddenly, your bank account gets debited. Sometimes, in multiple payments!

We have heard stories of this happening. A child spent thousands of rupees on a game. The parents were shocked. They didn't even know their child had access to their card details. It's easy for kids to get carried away. They want to win, they want to show off. And these game companies make it very easy to spend money. It's a tough situation. Because for kids, it might just be a game. But in actuality, it's real money.

Predatory Individuals: This is a very serious matter. In online games, kids often chat with other players. Some of these players are not youngsters, they are adults. And some of them have bad intentions. They pretend to be kids and talk sweetly to become 'friends' with your child.

They might ask personal questions: 'Where do you live?', 'Which school do you go to?', 'What's your full name?' Slowly, they try to build trust. Then, they might ask for photos. Or they might ask your child to meet them.

It's truly scary to think about. Our children are innocent. They trust easily. These bad people can manipulate that innocence. We need to be very, very careful about who our children are talking to online, because it's the equivalent of letting your child play in a park with strangers. If we would be wary of that in real life, then we should be careful online too.

Exposure to Inappropriate Content

The internet is a vast place; there is good content, but there is also very bad content. Our children can stumble upon things they should not see, things that are not meant for their age.

Sometimes, it's by accident. They search for something innocent, but a pop-up ad appears. Or a link leads them to a disturbing website. Other times, friends might share inappropriate videos or pictures on messaging apps.

Watching such content can be very damaging for a child. It can scare them, confuse them or even normalise bad behaviour. At an age where they are still developing, any exposure to media that is difficult for them to process can be damaging in the long term.

Sharing Personal Information

Children don't always understand the value of privacy. For them, sharing is caring. They might share their name, age, school's name, phone number or even home address with strangers online. They might do it to make new friends. Or to win a prize in a fake contest.

Cyber criminals love this. This information is gold for them. With a child's name and school, they can find out more. They can try to meet the child. They can even try to trick parents. It is possible that they call you and say, 'Your child is in trouble at school. We need money.' Because they know details about your child, you might believe them.

There was a case where a child shared their school's name and a photo of their house online. A criminal used this to pretend to be a delivery person and tried to enter the house. Luckily, the parents were alert. But it was a close call and could've resulted in a bad situation.

What Can Be Done

So, what do we do? Do we ban them from using the internet? That's not practical in today's world. The internet is here to stay. What we need is to teach them how to be safe. We need to be their guides.

Parental Controls: Many devices and apps have parental control settings. Please use them.

- ❖ Set Screen Time Limits: Decide how long your child can use the phone or computer. Their safety increases as their time on the internet decreases.
- ❖ Filter Content: Use settings that block inappropriate websites.
- ❖ App Permissions: Check what permissions games and apps ask for. Does a game really need access to your camera? Probably not.
- ❖ Password Protect Purchases: Make sure your credit card details are not easily accessible for in-game purchases. Use passwords for every transaction.
- ❖ Monitor Activity: Keep a tentative eye on what your children are doing online. Not to spy, but to guide. See which games they play, which websites they visit.

Open Communication: The most important tool is to talk to your children, honestly and often.

- Explain the Dangers: Tell them, in simple words, about the bad people online. Use stories to explain. 'Just like we don't talk to strangers on the road, we don't talk to strangers online.'
- Encourage Sharing: Tell them, 'If anything makes you feel uncomfortable online, tell me. No matter what. I will not get angry. I will help you.' Make them feel safe enough to share things with you.
- Discuss Privacy: Teach them what personal information is, and why they should never share it with anyone online. Their full name, address, phone number, information about their school, all of these are private details.
- Be a Digital Buddy: Play games with them sometimes. Explore websites together. This way, you understand their online world. And they feel like you are a part of it too.
- Lead by Example: If you are always on your phone, they will observe that, and possibly do the same. Show them a balanced use of technology.

Remember, children are curious. They learn by doing. Which is why we need to guide them. We need to be their trusted adults in the digital world. It's a continuous effort, and an important one. Because ensuring the safety of our children is crucial.

SENIORS: OUR WISDOM, THEIR VULNERABILITY

Let's talk about our seniors: our grandparents and other elderly family members. The digital world is often new to them. They might not have grown up with computers and smartphones and this newness can make them targets. Cyber criminals know their vulnerabilities and use clever tricks to exploit their trust. We have discussed many stories of these scams in earlier chapters. I think it is important to reiterate these scams for clarity. Cyber criminals mostly use these tricks to target our seniors.

Digital Arrest Scams: Seniors easily get into this frightening trap. Imagine an elder family member getting a call. The caller says, 'I am from the CBI.' Or 'I am from the police.' They use strong official language and elaborate props like police uniforms, background photos, fake arrest warrants, etc. Sometimes they even have a police siren sound in the background.

They tell our seniors, 'You have been involved in illegal activity.' Or 'There is a warrant for your arrest.' Or 'Your bank account has been used for money laundering.' This creates instant panic. Our seniors are law-abiding citizens. They get very scared. Then, the scammer says, 'To avoid arrest, you need to transfer money to a "safe" government account.' Or 'You need to buy gift cards and give us the codes.' They threaten them, saying, 'Don't tell anyone, or you will be arrested immediately!'

Seniors, frightened by this, often do what they are told. They transfer their hard-earned savings. They might even go to the bank multiple times. And the scammers keep calling. They don't stop until they have taken everything.

Sextortion: This is a truly troubling scam. It usually starts on social media or dating apps. The scammer pretends to be an attractive person. They connect with our seniors, often to build a relationship online. They flatter them and make them feel special.

Then, they ask for intimate pictures or videos. Or they might record the elder during a video call without their knowledge. Once they have this content, the blackmail begins.

They say, 'If you don't pay me money, I will send this video to your family. To your friends. To your office!' They threaten to expose them. In such situations, our seniors can feel immense shame or fear public humiliation. They must be scared of what their family will think. So, they pay. And pay. But the demands never stop.

This scam can cause deep emotional distress and leave a lasting scar. Seniors are often too ashamed to tell anyone, which can make them even more vulnerable.

Investment Scams: Seniors often worry about their retirement savings. They want to live comfortably in their old age. Scammers know this and offer fake investment opportunities.

They might call or send messages. 'Invest in this new cryptocurrency! It will double your money in a week!' Or 'Join this scheme! Get 30 per cent returns every month!' They create fake websites, show fake testimonials and pressure seniors into investing quickly. 'Limited time offers! Don't miss out!'

Initially, they might show small returns to build trust. Seniors might think, 'Wow, this is real!', and invest more.

Then suddenly, one day, the website disappears. The phone numbers are disconnected. All the money is gone.

These scams steal their life savings. The money meant for their medical needs. For their daily expenses.

Lottery/Prize Scams: This is an old scam, but it can still work. Especially with our seniors who might be less digitally savvy. They get an email, a message, or a call saying, 'Congratulations! You have won a lottery of ₹5 crore!' Or, 'You have won a brand new car!' Or, 'You are the lucky winner of a huge cash prize from a foreign country!'

The catch? 'To claim your prize, you just need to pay a small processing fee.' Or, 'You need to pay taxes first.' They ask for a few thousand rupees. Then, they ask for more for 'insurance', and 'certificate fees'. And it never stops.

Seniors can get excited by this and dream of how this money will change their lives. They pay the fees, but the prize never comes. Only more demands for money. And eventually, they realise they have been cheated. But by this time, their money is gone.

Emotional Scams: This is a particularly cruel scam. The scammer calls an elder person. They pretend to be their grandchild, or they say, 'I am calling on behalf of your grandchild.' They create an urgent situation: 'I've been arrested!', 'I had an accident!' or 'I lost my wallet in another city!' Sometimes scammers use deepfake, AI-generated videos to make these calls more believable.

They say, 'Don't tell mom and dad! They will be so angry!' These requests play on the grandparents' love and desire to protect their grandchild. They feel a sense of urgency and believing the caller, want to help immediately.

The scammer asks for money: 'I need ₹50,000 for bail!' Or 'I need money for medical treatment!' They tell the elder to send money through untraceable methods like gift cards or money transfer services.

Our seniors, driven by love and fear for their grandchild, send the money. Only to find out later that their grandchild was safe all along. The emotional toll of this scam can be immense.

What Can Be Done

So, what do we do? We can't unplug them from the internet. But protecting our seniors is paramount. Here are some ways in which we can help them.

- Patience Is Key: When talking to them about these scams, be patient. Don't scold them, they might feel embarrassed. Empathise with them. 'I understand this new technology can be confusing. It's not your fault.'
- If It Sounds Too Good to Be True, It Probably Is: Teach them this simple rule. Winning a lottery they didn't enter? A quick and huge return on investment? That's a scam.
- Never Share Personal Information Over the Phone/ Email: Tell them clearly: 'No bank, no government office, no police will ever ask for your passwords, OTPs or bank details over the phone or email. Never share this information.'
- Verify, Verify, Verify: If they get a call claiming to be from the bank, police or a family member asking for money, tell them: 'Hang up. Call the bank's official number.

Call the police station directly. Call your grandchild directly on their usual number. Do not trust the number they called you from.'

- Beware of Urgency and Threats: Scammers always create urgency and threaten people. Tell your seniors: 'If someone pressures you to act quickly, or threatens you, it's a scam. No legitimate organisation will do that.'
- No Remote Access: Explain 'Never allow anyone to access your computer remotely unless it's a trusted person you know and have called yourself for help.'
- Discuss Online Friendships: Gently explain that not everyone online is who they say they are. Be wary of strangers asking for money or intimate things.
- Share Scam Stories: Talk about these scams in a general way. 'Did you hear about that new scam where ...' This helps them recognise the patterns without feeling targeted.
- Set Up Alerts: If possible, set up SMS alerts for bank transactions on their phone. This way, they know if money is unexpectedly debited.
- Be Accessible: Make sure they feel comfortable calling you for any suspicious calls or messages. 'If you ever get a strange call or message, call me first. Let's check it together.'

We've seen why our children and our seniors need an extra hand to protect themselves online. These cyber threats are real, and scammers are always looking for easy targets. It's on us to keep talking to our children about what's safe and what's not, and to guide our seniors gently through the digital world. By staying alert, informed and communicating well, we can build a strong shield against scammers together.

Part Four

FORTIFYING YOUR DIGITAL WORLD: PRACTICAL STEPS

CHAPTER TEN

Protecting from 'Digital Pests'

Understanding the dangerous world of cybercrime, its tricks and targets, is the crucial first step. But, after knowing what the problems are, it is time to understand how we can protect ourselves, and you do not need to be a tech expert to do that! You only need to know a few simple, smart steps that anyone, from a school student to a grandparent, can follow.

In order to learn how to defend ourselves, we must thoroughly know the 'digital pests' we are dealing with. These can sneak into your phone, computer or laptop and cause a lot of trouble. We call them 'malware'.

The same way that insects enter our homes and spread disease or damage things, in the digital world, small software programs get into our devices and harm them. They can delete files, steal data or make a device incredibly slow. The smartest way to tackle them is by understanding what they are and how they work.

WHAT ARE THESE 'DIGITAL PESTS'?

You can think of malware as an unwanted guest that sneaks into your phone or computer to cause trouble. It comes in different forms like viruses, Trojans, spyware, ransomware and adware. Let's understand each type simply so you know what to watch out for.

Viruses, the Digital Cold: These are like a digital cold. They spread in your device, copying themselves and sticking to files. Viruses can slow your computer or ruin files. They often enter from bad email attachments, infected pen drives or risky websites. If your device has been acting weird, it might be a virus.

Trojans, the Sneaky Pretenders: These look like harmless apps or games but hide danger inside. Once downloaded, Trojans secretly let hackers into your device. This allows them to steal your passwords, bank details or even control your device. Always be careful before downloading new apps.

Spyware, the Silent Watcher: This malware secretly enters your device and spies on everything. Spyware records what you type, the websites you visit or the apps that you use, and forwards this data to criminals.

Ransomware, the Digital Kidnapper: This locks your family photos or important files. A scary message pops up demanding money, or your files are gone! Ransomware enters through fake emails or risky downloads. Even if you pay, there's no guarantee that you'll get your files back.

Adware, the Annoying Pop-Up Pest: This malware bothers you with endless ads—pop-ups and new tabs everywhere! Adware often hides in free apps or on certain websites and can slow down your device or track your browsing history. While it is annoying, it can also be risky, sometimes leading to worse malware or sharing your information.

'DIGITAL PEST' CONTROL

Now know about these digital pests, we must learn the ways to do damage control. It's not difficult. It's just about developing good habits to keep your computer clean and safe.

Your Digital Pest Control

Install and use an antivirus: this is your first line of defence, your digital pest control. A good antivirus software constantly scans your computer for malware. It can detect, block and remove viruses, Trojans, spyware and even ransomware.

- Make sure you have a reputable antivirus installed on your computer and even on your Android phone (for iPhones, the risk is lower but it is still good to have one).
- Keep it updated. New malware is created every single day. Your antivirus needs to know about these new threats to protect you. So, ensure that your antivirus updates automatically.
- Run regular scans on your devices. Schedule full scans of your system regularly, at least once a week.

- Don't ignore notifications from your antivirus. They are there to help you!

Vaccinations for Your Devices

Just like we get vaccinations to protect ourselves from diseases, your software and operating system (Windows, macOS, Android, iOS) need regular updates to protect themselves. Your system updates often include 'security patches' that are crucial.

- Security Patches: These are fixes for weak spots or 'holes' in the software that cyber criminals could exploit to sneak in malware.
- Enable Automatic Updates: Most operating systems and popular software (like your web browser, Microsoft Office) have an option for automatic updates. Enable it! It's the easiest way to stay protected.
- Don't Ignore Update Notifications: When your phone or computer says 'Update available', don't say 'Oh, another update? Later.' Do it as soon as possible.
- Be Careful with USB Drives: Never plug in just any pen drive, especially if you do not know where it came from. Always scan any USB drive with your antivirus software before you open any files on it. This can stop viruses from infiltrating.

Don't Open Unknown Gifts

Always be careful with downloads and email attachments. This is where most infections happen, like the Trojan Horse.

- Only Download from Trusted Sources: If you need software, an app or a game, download it from the official website or reputable app stores (Google Play Store, Apple App Store). Avoid downloading from random websites or pirated software sites or through a WhatsApp message sent by someone. These are breeding grounds for malware.
- Think Before You Click on Email Attachments: If you receive an email with an attachment from someone you don't know, or if it looks suspicious even though you received it from someone you know (e.g., a strange subject line, bad grammar), do not open it. Many tricky emails, called 'phishing' emails, often carry viruses or ransomware.
- Verify the Sender: If you're unsure about an email from a known contact, call them or message them separately to confirm that they sent it. In a mobile phone, verifying sender email takes some effort. The display name may be fake.
- Be Wary of Shortened Links: Links that look like bit.ly/xyz or tinyurl.com/abc can hide dangerous destinations. These are short links or aliases. They are not real sites. Be cautious.
- Learn to Spot Scams: If you get a message saying your files are locked or that you've visited a pornography site, and it's demanding money, do not panic and never pay. First, disconnect your device from the internet immediately. Then, run an antivirus scan and ask for help from a trusted tech expert.

Your Digital Security Guard

A firewall is like a security guard standing at the entrance of your home network. It monitors all incoming and outgoing internet traffic. It blocks suspicious connections and prevents unauthorised access to your computer. Most operating systems (Windows, macOS) have a built-in firewall. Make sure it's turned on. It's an important layer of defence, silently protecting your device.

Don't Fall for the Bait

Adware is annoying, but it can also be dangerous.

- Don't Click on Suspicious Pop-Ups: If a pop-up appears saying 'Your computer is infected! Click here to clean it!'—it's probably a scam trying to get you to download malware. Close it immediately.
- Use an Ad Blocker: For your web browser, you can install a good ad blocker extension. This can prevent many annoying ads and pop-ups from appearing, reducing the risk of malware.
- Close Pop-Ups Correctly: Often, the 'X' button on a pop-up might be fake. Look for the real 'X' or just close the browser tab.

Back Up Your Important Data

This is not a prevention method, but a recovery method. Even with all the precautions, sometimes things can go wrong. If you get hit by ransomware, and you have a backup of your important files, you can simply wipe your system clean and restore your data from the backup. That way, you don't have to pay the ransom. Think of it like having an emergency fund.

- Regular Backups: Back up your photos, documents, videos and other important files regularly.
- External Drive or Cloud Storage: Use an external hard drive or a reputable cloud storage service (like Google Drive, OneDrive, iCloud, Dropbox) for backups.
- Offline Backups: For critical data, consider keeping a backup copy on an external drive that you disconnect from your computer after the backup is complete. This protects it from online threats like ransomware.

Malware, ransomware and adware are real threats that can cause a lot of trouble. But now that you know what they are and how they work, you can protect yourself. The same way you lock the doors to your house, you need to secure your digital doors too.

CHAPTER ELEVEN

Passwords Are the 'Key'

Antivirus software is our first line of defence to stay safe online. Our next line of defence is something we all use every single day: passwords.

We use them for everything important: emails, bank accounts, social media. They are the keys to our digital home. They keep our online information safe. Which is why we need to make sure that our digital keys are strong.

STRONG AND UNIQUE PASSWORDS

If you have only one key for your home, your office and your locker, and someone gets access to that one key, everything is compromised! That is the same case with passwords. If you use the same password everywhere, it can be very risky for your online safety.

Cyber criminals are clever; they find ways to guess passwords, and use special programs to crack them. These programs go through millions of combinations and a weak password is easy to crack. On the contrary, a strong password is like a solid steel door. It takes a lot of time and effort to break open. Most criminals will just move on to look for easier targets.

The key word here is 'unique'. If a website you use gets hacked, and you have used the same password elsewhere, like your bank account, that account is now at risk. It's like putting all your eggs in one basket, which can make you digitally vulnerable

Creating Memorable and Secure Passwords

'But how do I remember so many strong passwords?' This is a common question. It seems tough, but there are some smart methods.

- Make It Long: The longer, the better. Aim for at least twelve to fifteen characters.
- Use a Phrase, Not a Word: Don't use your name, or your birth date, or 'password123'. These are too common. Think of a sentence: a line from your favourite song, a funny memory. For example, 'Sheru loves to bark!' This is easy for you to remember. Now, turn it into a password: *Sh3ruL0v3sT0B@rk!* It's long, it has numbers, it has symbols, it's unique.
- Mix It Up: Use a mix of things—small letters, capital letters, numbers, special symbols. Consider *MyS3cr3tP@ssw0rd!* It looks messy. That's good!
- Don't Use Personal Info: Your pet's name, your phone number, your address. These are easy to find online. Criminals will know to look for this information.
- Avoid Dictionary Words: Don't use words like 'apple' or 'computer'. Programs can guess these easily.

- Use a Password Manager: This is a fantastic tool. It's an app or software. It creates strong passwords for you, and remembers them too. You only need one master password for the manager. A good option for Chrome users is Google Password Manager.

ADDITIONAL AUTHENTICATION

This feature is a game-changer. It is an extra lock on your door. Even if someone gets your password, they still can't get in. They need something else, the second factor. That's why it's called 'two-factor' or 'multi-factor' authentication.

Here is how it works: after you type your password, the system asks for a second key. This second key could be:

- A Code Sent to Your Phone: You get an SMS with a special code and you type that code to get in.
- Device Features: A fingerprint or face scan.
- A Code from an Authenticator App: Apps like Google Authenticator or Microsoft Authenticator generate a new code every thirty to sixty seconds. This code needs to be typed in after the password is entered. It is linked to your device.
- A Physical Security Key: A small device you plug into your computer. This is rarely used for personal use, but companies often use this.

The extra step for authentication makes hacking much, much harder. Even if a criminal gets your password, they don't have your phone or your fingerprint. This extra step provides a lot of security.

For Common Accounts

Most major online services offer MFA: your email provider (Gmail, Outlook), your bank, social media platforms (Facebook, Instagram) and even online shopping sites (Amazon, Flipkart). You can usually enable it through your account settings:

- Go to your account settings.
- Find the security or privacy section.
- Look for Two Factor Authentication /Verification or Multi-Factor Authentication
- The app or website will guide you further. You might need to add your phone number. Or download an authenticator app.

Take some time today to enable MFA on your most important accounts: your email, your bank, your primary social media. This is a very powerful step you can take, and it will protect you much more.

Protecting yourself online is not just about big attacks; it is about taking small, smart steps every day. Strong passwords are key, and using different ones for different accounts is vital. MFA adds another very important layer of security. Always turn it on if you can. Your digital life is important, and it is definitely worth protecting.

CHAPTER TWELVE

Smart Habits for Every Family Member

There is something even more important than managing malware and making strong passwords: our daily actions online. Just like we have good habits for our health, we also need smart habits for using the internet. These are simple, everyday things that keep us safe from cyber threats and these can be practiced by everyone—our kids, parents and grandparents. Let's learn these habits to use the internet safely.

EMAIL

Every day, we get many emails, from friends, from companies, but some can be from cyber thieves. But how do we know who is who?

First, check who sent the email. Look at the sender's email address which contains an '@' symbol, not the display name. Does it look strange? For example, your bank's email won't be '*bank.alerts.123@gmail.com*'. It will be something official, such as '*noreply@onlinesbi.sbi*' or '*info@hdfcbank.com*'. If it looks weird, be wary of it. Viewing emails on a phone may be difficult but you must check nonetheless.

Next, look at the subject line. Does it say something like 'Urgent Action Required!' or 'Your Account Is Suspended!'? These are often tricks, they want you to panic and quickly click on the tricky link or attachment. Be patient, don't fall for it.

These emails often carry links, those blue words that redirect you to another page. Cyber thieves often put malicious ones in their emails. If you click on them, they can take over your computer, or steal your information. So, before you click, hover your mouse over the link. Don't click, just move your mouse on top. You will see the actual link address. Does it look genuine? Link display text may be different from the actual link address. If the email says it's from Amazon, but the link is to '*superdiscount.xyz*', then it's a trap. Don't click on such links. It's better to go directly to the website. Open a new tab and type the website address yourself. This is always safer.

And what about spam? Those unwanted emails that fill up our inbox. Most email services have a 'Spam' or 'Junk' folder. Be sure to use it. If you see a spam email, mark it as spam. This helps your email service learn. Next time you receive such an email, it will send it the spam folder directly. Alternatively, you can block senders.

Remember, if something in an email feels off, trust your gut feeling. Don't click. Don't reply. Just delete it.

SOCIAL MEDIA

We all share our lives on social media: our photos, our videos, our thoughts, our holidays. But the important thing to remember is that not everyone on social media is your friend. Some people are looking for information. They want to use it against you for their own gain.

The first thing to understand are privacy settings. Most social media platforms let you choose who sees your posts. Set your profile to 'Friends Only' or 'Private'. Don't make it 'Public'. It is safer to share your information with people you know and trust.

A crucial skill is identifying fake profiles. You might get a friend request from someone you don't know, or someone who looks too good to be true. Look at their profile. Do they have very few friends? Are all their photos stock images? Do they post very little? These are red flags indicating that the profile could be fake. They might be trying to trick you, maybe to get your information or to send you a bad link. If in doubt, don't accept the request.

We must understand what you should avoid sharing. Never share your full address, or your phone number publicly. Don't post pictures of your airline tickets, or your boarding pass. These have important details that thieves can use. Be wary of posting about your holiday plans. For example, saying, 'Hey! Off to Goa for a week!' tells thieves your house is empty. Think before you post. Ask yourself: 'Do I really want everyone to know this?'

Every photo you post, every check-in at a restaurant, every comment you make, it all adds up. It creates a picture of your life, and sometimes, this picture can be used against you. Imagine you post a picture of your child in their school uniform, with the school's logo clearly visible. Now, anyone can find out where your child goes to school. This is dangerous. Or you constantly post about your daily routine. Things like, 'Just leaving for work!' or 'Finally home after a long day!' This tells criminals when your house is empty.

Think carefully about your privacy, your family's privacy and evaluate your safety. Before you post, ask: 'Be mindful, be smart.

ONLINE SHOPPING

Online shopping is very convenient; from clothes to groceries, everything is just a click away. But this can also be dangerous, scammers can put up fake websites and unsafe payment portals.

In such cases, reviews are crucial. Before buying anything online, check reviews of the website and the product. Use Google Search to look for public sources and don't trust reviews on the same website. Verify if Google has good reviews, and if they seem genuine. If a website has no reviews, or only very few, be cautious.

Next, know which ones are secure payment methods. Always use trusted payment routes, such as net banking, UPI or your credit/debit card. Avoid direct bank transfers to unknown sellers. Credit cards often offer more protection. If something goes wrong, you can dispute the charge. Never share your card's CVV (three-digit secure code) or PIN with anyone. Not even if someone calls you claiming to be from your bank. Your bank will never ask for these details.

Enter payment details like credit card details, or net banking ones only on trusted payment gateways. Verify the URL of the payment screen. It should be that of your bank, a reputed payment gateway's or a reputed site. Fraudsters use fake payment pages to collect your payment information, and they use that in other sites to take away your money.

Think logically when shopping online. If something sounds too good, it's most likely a scam, and safer to just ignore.

DOWNLOAD

We often download apps, movies, songs, documents, books on our devices. But where do you download them from? We must be very careful about this.

Only download from trusted sources. For apps, use the official app stores, such as Google Play Store for Android or Apple App Store for iPhones. For software, always go to the company's official website. Don't download from random websites, or from links in emails. These downloads can contain viruses or malware. They can harm your computer and even steal your information. Hackers can corrupt these downloads with malicious code.

It's very straightforward; we buy our food from a clean, trusted place, and it's the same for downloads. You should only get them from trusted places.

DEVICES

Your digital life doesn't just live in the cloud. It lives on your devices too: your phone, your laptop, even your smart TV. They all need protection. In this section we will discuss a few ways to secure our digital world.

Secure Wi-Fi Networks

Your home Wi-Fi is your private connection to the internet. When you set up your Wi-Fi, make sure it has a strong password, just like your other passwords. Use a mix of letters, numbers and symbols. Don't use 'admin' or 'password'. Be sure to change the default password given by your internet provider.

Avoid public Wi-Fi for sensitive tasks. Those free Wi-Fi spots at cafes, airports, railway stations and hotels are often not secure. Anyone can be on that network. A cybercriminal could be watching your data.

- Never do banking on public Wi-Fi.
- Never log into sensitive accounts.
- If you must use public Wi-Fi, please use Virtual Private Network (VPN) software. A VPN encrypts your data. It creates a secure tunnel. But for most sensitive things, just wait until you are on a secure network. Your personal mobile data is usually safer than public Wi-Fi.

Managing App Permissions

The various apps on your phones often ask for 'permissions', like access to your contacts, your text messages, your camera, your location, your call logs, your microphone, etc.

'Allow' or 'Deny'? We often tap 'Allow' without thinking. But it is safer to pause and consider, does a flashlight app really need access to your contacts? Does a simple game need your location all the time? Probably not.

- Be Mindful When Installing Apps: Look at the permissions the app asks for. If it seems too much, be careful. Maybe find another app.
- Review Permissions Regularly: On your phone, go to 'Settings' -> 'Apps' or 'App Management', There, you can see what permissions each app has. Turn off anything that seems unnecessary or suspicious. You must review apps which access your contacts, text messages and call logs.

This helps protect your privacy and stops apps from secretly collecting your data.

Secure Disposal of Old Devices

When you buy a new phone, be careful of what you do with the old one. Don't just throw it in the dustbin or sell it without cleaning it properly. Your old device might still have your personal data: your photos, your messages, your bank details.

Before disposing of an old device:

- Back Up Your Important Data: Transfer all your photos, documents, contacts to your new device or a cloud service.
- Factory Reset: This is crucial. A factory reset wipes all your data from the device. On most phones, it's in

'Settings' -> 'System' or 'General Management' -> 'Reset Options' -> 'Erase all data (factory reset)'.

- ❖ Remove All Accounts: Before resetting, make sure you are logged out of all your accounts (Google, Apple ID, etc.).

These steps ensure that your old data doesn't fall into the wrong hands. It's the digital equivalent of shredding old documents.

These smart habits—managing emails, social media, online shopping, downloads and device security—are simple, yet powerful. Teach them to your children, share them with your parents and weave them into your daily routine.

CHAPTER THIRTEEN

Immediate Actions for Recovery

It can be very unfortunate if you or someone you know falls prey to a scam. What matters is what can be done next.

It's important to take action, and quick ones. Scams are like a fire. You need to put it out fast. Every second counts.

FINANCIAL FRAUD

This is often the most harmful. Hard-earned money is gone, or it's about to be.

- Call your bank immediately. This is the first thing you must do. Find their emergency helpline number. It's usually on your ATM card or credit card. Or on their website. Many banks have a 24/7 helpline. They may be able to track where the money is gone, and it might be possible to block it before it is withdrawn.
- Tell your bank everything. Explain what happened, when it happened and the amount that was compromised. It is important to give them all the details.
- Block cards. If someone else used your debit card, credit card or even UPI, block it. Ask the bank to do it. This

stops any more unauthorised transactions. If they can't block it right away, ask them to hot-list it. This makes the card useless.

- Check bank statements. Ask your bank to check all recent transactions, look for anything you didn't authorise. Screenshot them if you can see them on your banking app. This can be used later as evidence.
- If it's UPI fraud, contact your UPI app provider too. Like Google Pay, PhonePe, Paytm. They might have a fraud reporting option.

In such cases the faster you act, the better your chances of getting the money back. It is best to be calm and reach out for help.

COMPROMISED ACCOUNT

Sometimes, what's lost is not money directly. But your online accounts, like your email, social media or even shopping accounts. These are also very important.

- Change Passwords Everywhere: If one account is hacked, assume others are at risk where you use the same password. Change the password for the hacked account first. Then, change passwords for those accounts where you have used the same password. Every account is important.
- Make Strong Passwords: Don't use your name. Or your birth date. Use a mix of small letters, capital letters, numbers and symbols. Make them long.

- Enable Two-Factor Authentication (2FA) or Multi-Factor Authentication (MFA): Even if someone has your password, they still need a second code to log in. This code usually comes to your phone. It's like a second lock on your door and it's very important.

MALWARE INFECTION

This one is for a specific type of attack: malware, or ransomware.

- Disconnect from the internet immediately. If you see strange things happening on your computer, like files getting locked, weird pop-ups or your computer slowing down a lot, pull out the internet cable, or switch off your Wi-Fi. This stops the malware from spreading. It also stops it from sending your data to the hacker.
- Do not pay the ransom. I know you just want your files back, but paying them can often makes things worse. They might not give you the key, or they might ask for more money.
- Get expert help. If your computer is infected, take it to a trusted computer repair shop. Or a cyber security expert. They can help clean it.

COLLECTING EVIDENCE

This part is very important for reporting the crime: you need proof.

- Take Screenshots: If get a fake SMS or a suspicious email, take a screenshot. If you see a fraudulent transaction on your banking app, screenshot it.
- Save Messages and Emails: If the fraudster contacted you via WhatsApp, Telegram or email, save those chats. Don't delete them. They are valuable clues.
- Note Down Transaction Details: If money was lost, write down the date, time, amount and the account where the money went (if you know it).
- Keep All Communication Records: Any calls you made to the bank should be notes down. Record details of the time and who you spoke to.
- Don't Alter Anything: Don't change the screenshots, don't edit the messages, keep them as they are. This makes them more credible.

These clues will help the police and get your complaint addressed faster.

REPORTING CYBERCRIME

You've taken immediate actions. Now, it's time to report the crime. This is your right, and it's your duty too.

Helpline 1930 for Financial Fraud

This number is a helpline used specifically for financial fraud.

- When to use 1930? Use it immediately for financial fraud, especially if money has just been debited from your account, or if you have been tricked into sending money.

- Call 1930. This is a toll-free number. It connects you to the National Cybercrime Helpline.
- Provide details quickly, they will ask for your name, phone number, bank name, amount lost and time of transaction.
- Why is 1930 important? This helpline works with banks and payment wallets. If you report quickly, they can try to freeze the money movement, they can even try to reverse the transaction. This is why immediate action is key. The faster you call, the better the chances of getting your money back.
- You still need to file an online complaint. After calling 1930, they will usually ask you to also file a detailed complaint on *cybercrime.gov.in*. The call is for immediate action. The online complaint is for formal investigation.

National Cybercrime Reporting Portal

This is the main place to report cybercrime in India. It's a government portal and easy to use.

- Go to *cybercrime.gov.in*. This is the official website. Be careful, there are fake websites too. Make sure it has '.gov.in'.
- Click on 'File a Complaint'. You will see options: 'Report other cybercrime' or 'Report financial fraud'. Choose the one that fits your situation. Read the terms and conditions, and accept them.
- Register yourself. You will need to create an account using your mobile number.

- Fill in the details. This is where all your evidence comes in handy. Victim details: your name, contact number, address. Incident details: when did it happen? Where? What kind of crime? Suspect details (if you have any): any phone number? Email ID? UPI ID? Account number?
- Upload all your screenshots, messages, transaction details.
- Review and submit. Check all details carefully before submitting.
- Get an acknowledgement number. Once you submit, you will get a unique complaint ID. Keep this safely. You will need it to track your complaint.

It's important to capture all necessary information. Take your time and fill it correctly.

Contacting Local Police/Cyber Cell

Sometimes you might also need to visit the police station.

- For Serious Cases: If it's a very large amount, or if you fear for your safety, or if the online portal is not working for some reason, it is better to visit the police station.
- File a Cybercrime Complaint: Ask for the cyber cell. Many larger police stations have a dedicated cyber cell. These are police officers trained in cybercrime.
- Take All Your Evidence: Show them your screenshots, messages, complaint ID from the portal (if you filed one).
- Get a Copy of the FIR: When they register your complaint, it's called an FIR (First Information Report). Insist on getting a copy of the FIR. This is your official record.

Prompt reporting for cybercrimes is absolutely critical. It gives you the best possible chance of recovery.

- Prevents Further Harm: If it's an account hack, reporting quickly helps lock down your accounts. It stops the hacker from doing more harm.
- Helps Investigation: The fresher the crime, the more clues that are available. Call records, IP addresses, transaction trails are easier to trace right after the incident.
- Helps Others: Every report helps the police understand how these criminals work. It helps them track down gangs. Your report might save someone else from falling victim.

DON'T FEEL ASHAMED

Many people feel embarrassed or ashamed after falling victim to cybercrime. They question how they could have been foolish enough to fall prey to a scam. But it is important to remember that these criminals are professional deceivers. They target everyone, from youngsters to elders. It's not a sign of your weakness. It's a sign of their cunning. Don't let shame stop you from reporting. Reporting helps you, and it helps others.

The details in this chapter are an emergency kit. If you find yourself in such a terrible situation, remember that resources and help are always available. Take the given steps, be vigilant and be cyber smart.

Conclusion

A SAFER DIGITAL FUTURE FOR YOUR FAMILY

Throughout the book, we've explored various corners of the digital world and its dangers. This world can feel vast and overwhelming, but learning about it thoroughly is the first step to protecting yourself digitally.

What We've Learned Together

Let's do an overview of the concepts discussed in the book.

- Personal Information: It is extremely important to keep your personal information, like your Aadhaar card details, PAN or bank account numbers, truly private. These are like your house keys; it is not safe to give them to just anyone.
- Phishing: These are sneaky messages, emails or calls that try to trick you into giving away your secrets.
- Fake Phone or Video Calls: These can often be used to scam us. Always double-check. If something feels too good to be true, it probably is.
- Fake Online Investments: Putting your money into fake online investments, shopping and cryptocurrency

platforms can be dangerous. It's convenient, but we need to be careful about where we buy things from, where we invest and what payment methods we use. Stick to trusted websites and apps always.

- Risks of Social Media: It's important to stay connected, but social media can also be a place where wrongdoers try to reach you or your children.
- Strong Passwords: This cannot be just your birthday. Make your passwords lengthy and complex.
- OTP Messages: They are extremely important. Be careful and read the full text of OTP messages. Never share them with anyone, no matter what they say.
- Protecting Our Children Online: This is important and serious. Our kids are growing up with phones and tablets, and it's our job to guide them to use these devices safely. The key is to have open communication, not just strict rules. They should feel comfortable coming to you, no matter what.

You Have the Power

All this knowledge isn't just for learning; it's for using too. Understanding how scams work shouldn't scare you off the internet; it should teach you how to be smart about it. Think of it like learning how to drive. You don't stop driving because there are accidents; you learn the rules of the road and drive carefully.

Being aware is half the battle won. You now know what to look out for. And the other half? It's taking proactive measures. This means taking action before something bad happens, like regularly updating your phone and computer software, or setting up privacy settings on your social media accounts. It means having conversations with your family about online safety, not just once, but on a regular basis.

The internet is always changing, and so are the ways people try to misuse it. Thus, staying informed is crucial. Read the news, talk to others.

Stay smart. Stay secure. And always keep learning and sharing. Because together, we can make the digital world a safer place for everyone.

Appendices

A: CHECKLISTS FOR YOUR SAFETY

Device Security Checklist

- Keep Software Updated: Are your phone's software, computer's operating system (Windows/macOS), and apps always updated? (Yes/No)
- Antivirus Installed and Updated: Do you have good antivirus software on your computer and phone? Is it always updated? (Yes/No)
- Strong Passwords: Do you use different, strong passwords for all your important accounts? (Yes/No)
- Two-Factor/Multi-Factor Authentication (2FA/MFA): Is 2FA/MFA turned on for your email, banking and social media accounts? (Yes/No)
- Screen Lock: Do you use a password, PIN, pattern, or fingerprint lock on your phone and computer? (Yes/No)
- Public Wi-Fi Caution: Do you avoid doing banking or shopping on public Wi-Fi? (Yes/No)
- Back Up Data: Do you regularly back up your important photos and documents that are present on your phone and computer? (Yes/No)

Online Transactions Checklist

- Secure Website (HTTPS): Before paying, do you check if the website address starts with 'https://' and has a padlock symbol? (Yes/No)
- Verify URL: Do you verify the domain name of the website carefully before entering any data? (Yes/No)
- OTP Verification: Do you always read the full OTP message details before using the OTP on any app or website? (Yes/No)
- Trusted Seller: Are you buying from a well-known and trusted website or app? Do you do enough research if you are buying for the first time from any website? (Yes/No)
- Avoid Clicking Links in Messages: Do you directly type the website address instead of clicking links from unknown SMS or emails for payments? (Yes/No)
- Review Statements: Do you regularly check your bank and credit card statements for suspicious transactions? (Yes/No)

Social Media and Email Safety Checklist

- Privacy Settings: Have you checked and tightened your privacy settings on social media? (Yes/No)
- Think Before You Share: Do you think twice before sharing very personal information online? (Yes/No)
- Friend Requests from Strangers: Are you cautious about accepting friend requests from people you don't know? (Yes/No)
- Suspicious Links/Attachments: Do you avoid opening attachments or clicking links in suspicious emails or messages? (Yes/No)

- Verify Information: Do you cross-check any surprising news or offers received via email or social media through a trusted site? (Yes/No)

B: IMPORTANT CONTACT NUMBERS AND WEBSITES

- Helpline Number: 1930 (This is a nationwide helpline in India for cyber frauds related to money.)
- National Cybercrime Reporting Portal: www.cybercrime.gov.in
- Your Bank's Customer Care (Please fill in this page for your quick reference):

  ....

  ....

  ....

- Your Internet Service Provider (ISP) Customer Care (Please fill in this page for your quick reference):

  ....

  ....

  ....

Acknowledgements

To my wife, thank you for your pampering, which sustained me through every writing hour.

To my seniors and peers, your expertise and the learning opportunities you provided were fundamental to my growth as a cybersecurity specialist.

And to my friends and family, especially Sunny, your invaluable inputs in concept-shaping and continuous support were vital in bringing this book to help Indian families.